All About
JESUS

—

A FAMILY DEVOTIONAL

SHELBY TURNER

WHAT'S INSIDE

Extras

Section One

SEEING JESUS IN GENESIS–DEUTERONOMY

Section Two

SEEING JESUS IN JOSHUA–MALACHI

Section Three

SEEING JESUS IN MATTHEW–JOHN

Section Four

SEEING JESUS IN ACTS-REVELATION

"

LIKE ALL PEOPLE, CHILDREN HAVE *a deep inner desire* TO UNDERSTAND WHO GOD IS.

"

HEY, GROWN-UPS!

~~~~~~~~

We are thrilled that you have chosen to use the *All About Jesus Family Devotional* in your home. As parents, grandparents, and caregivers, we often think about the physical needs of the children in our lives. They need to be fed, clothed, and bathed. And their flourishing requires our attention, care, and love. But do we also consider their spiritual needs? Like all people, children have a deep inner desire to understand who God is, who they are, and for what purpose they have been created. They also experience the highs and lows of life and need a worldview that helps them understand the good and not-so-good things they experience. Our children desperately need to be taught who God is and what He has spoken to us through His Word.

Thankfully, the Bible gives us some instruction on how to handle this very daunting task! Deuteronomy 6:6–7 tells us the primary way children should be taught about the ways of God is not through pastors, children's ministries, or even churches but through families. Parents, guardians, and caregivers are the ones called to teach and train children about God and His ways. God told Moses to talk about the ways of God to children "when you sit in your house and when you walk along the road, when you lie down and when you get up" (Deuteronomy 6:7). Simply put, teaching children about God is a 24/7 job. It's as much a part of parenting as preparing daily meals for your children.

We have created the *All About Jesus Family Devotional* as a resource for you to use as you teach your children about God. This devotional focuses on teaching your children who Jesus is and what He has done for them. Each and every devotion covers a passage of Scripture and plainly explains how we can see Jesus and the good news of the gospel in that passage. You will also find memory verses, discussion questions, and prayer prompts to help your entire family engage more deeply with the content.

In addition, we have included a few helpful resources for you to consider as you begin this devotional with your family. These resources include: How to Make Time for Family Devotions, Overcoming Challenges, Tips for Helping Children Memorize Scripture, and Sharing the Gospel with Children.

We wholeheartedly believe that God will equip you to disciple the children in your life. It will not always be easy or look picture-perfect, but every minute, every verse, and every prayer counts. We pray God draws your children—and you—to Himself through this devotional. We are cheering you on!

God will equip you to disciple
the children in your life.

How to Make Time for
FAMILY DEVOTIONS

Family life is always busy! We are often juggling school, work, extracurricular activities, appointments, and so much more. How can we make time for family devotions in the midst of all that we have on our calendars? The answer may be more simple than you think. Below are three steps that will help you make the time!

Step 1: Pick a time.

On average, a devotion in the *All About Jesus Family Devotional* takes fifteen minutes to complete. When does your family have fifteen minutes to spare? Is it in the mornings before everyone takes off for work and school? During mealtime? In the car? Or before bed? Pick a time that will work best. It may not work perfectly every day, and that's okay. You may pick a time and then end up changing it when seasons and commitments change, and that's also okay. There is no such thing as the perfect time! Just start with what will work best for now, and remain flexible yet committed to your family devotion time.

Step 2: Communicate.

Let everyone in the family know you will be spending fifteen minutes a day doing a family devotion together at the time you have chosen. This may mean family members need to slightly alter their schedules to be present. Remember, the spiritual health of your family is important. Your children need this time, whether or not they realize it yet. It's okay to ask family members to reprioritize their time in order to read and study Scripture together.

Step 3: Follow Through.

Be sure that you follow through with your commitment to lead your family in a devotion. Even if everyone else comes begrudgingly, you can come passionately, knowing that the conversations you are about to have with your children will last for eternity. God speaks through His Word and His people. And He will speak to your children through Scripture, this devotional, and you. You can show up to your family's devotion time, knowing God has something to speak to you and your children!

If your family does not already have a daily family devotion time, you will be amazed by how quickly it becomes a normal part of your family life. Let's begin right now by filling out the questions on the next page.

The best time for my family to do a family devotion is

_____

_____ .

We will do family devotions

_____ times per week.

The challenges I foresee in making this time work are

_____

_____

_____ .

I will work to overcome these challenges by

_____

_____

_____

_____ .

We will do family devotions in
this location

We will begin on this date

The people in my family I need
to communicate this plan to are

Overcoming CHALLENGES

Below are some common challenges parents and caregivers face when teaching their children about God and the Bible. If and when you experience any of these, feel free to refer back to these pages for encouragement!

MY KIDS AREN'T PAYING ATTENTION. ARE THEY EVEN LEARNING ANYTHING?

Kids have very short attention spans and are easily distracted. We understand how that can make you wonder if it's even worth it to put effort into a family devotion time. It is not likely your kids will remember every little thing they are taught. But it is likely that they will remember something, and often they will recall more than you think!

Teaching children about God is a marathon, not a sprint. It's a race you will likely run alongside your children for decades. The goal isn't for your children to have perfect retention today but to faithfully and consistently teach them for a lifetime. Don't be discouraged by their wandering minds. Instead, be patient with them, trusting that even when they are distracted, it does not stop the Holy Spirit from working in their hearts and minds.

Scripture: Isaiah 55:10–11

I DON'T FEEL EQUIPPED TO TEACH THE BIBLE TO MY KIDS.

The Bible is a big, long, and sometimes confusing book. It's completely normal to feel intimidated by the task of teaching your children the truth it holds. Be encouraged that you do not need to be an expert to lead your family in the pursuit of God. It is okay if you feel confused about passages of Scripture or theological concepts. You can be honest with your children and say, "I'm not sure what that means, but we can figure it out together." A good study Bible would be a great place to start if you want to dive deeper into certain verses or concepts.

Scripture: 2 Peter 1:3, 1 Corinthians 11:1

MY SPOUSE AND I AREN'T ON THE SAME PAGE.

A common challenge to teaching children about God is when your spouse is not on the same page as you. They may be neutral or apathetic about faith conversations, or they may be completely opposed to them. While every family is different, and we cannot tell you how to handle this situation amid your unique family dynamics, there are a few things you may want to consider trying.

First, pray for unity between you and your spouse. Pray for the Holy Spirit to do a deep inner work in your spouse's heart and grow an affection for God and His Word in him or her. Second, let your spouse know about your plan for a family devotion time; invite them to take part in it, but do not pressure them to join. Third, be flexible. Your spouse may feel like your family devotion time is causing division in the family. Consider shortening your family devotion time or incorporating a non-faith-centric activity in which they can participate.

Scripture: 1 Corinthians 7:12–16

Teaching children about God is a marathon, not a sprint.

"
YOU DO NOT NEED
TO BE AN EXPERT
TO LEAD YOUR
FAMILY IN THE
pursuit of God.
"

Tips for Helping Children
MEMORIZE SCRIPTURE

+ Create actions to go along with each word or phrase.

+ Practice a few times a day. Some great times to practice are during meals, in the car, and before bed.

+ Write the first letter of each word in the verse on a sticky note, and use it as a cheat sheet until the verse is memorized.

+ Post the verse in a visible place like the bathroom mirror or refrigerator.

+ Sing the verse to the tune of a familiar song.

+ Have children look up the verse in the Bible and read it independently.

+ Keep track of verses memorized, and practice them once a week to promote long-term memory.

+ Use resources from The Daily Grace Co. such as the *Scripture Memory Journal* for kids or the *Daily He Leads Me* notepad for kids. You can find these resources at www.thedailygraceco.com.

Sharing the Good News of
THE GOSPEL WITH CHILDREN

Many people begin their relationship with Jesus at a young age. Throughout this devotional, the good news of the gospel is presented. Children may understand their sin and need for a Savior for the first time during this devotional. Grown-ups, you may want to ask your children if they want to decide to believe in Jesus and receive forgiveness for their sins. It is important not to pressure children to make this decision, but it is also important to lead them to Christ if they are ready.

We suggest asking your children the following questions to start a conversation about the gospel.

+ What do you think about today's devotion?

+ Do you think Jesus died to forgive your sins?

+ Are you ready to ask forgiveness for your sins and tell Jesus you believe in Him?

Listen to your child's answers, and encourage them if they say they want to repent and believe. If your child expresses their belief in Jesus and a desire to trust Him as their Savior, you may want to help them communicate their repentance and belief to God.

When your child is ready to respond to the gospel message, there is no specific prayer to pray or formula to follow. Interestingly, the Bible never actually presents us with a prayer that leads to salvation. Instead, Jesus often calls people to believe (John 6:35) and follow Him (Matthew 19:21). And the apostles teach us to "confess with your mouth, 'Jesus is Lord,' and believe in your heart that God raised him from the dead" to be saved (Romans 10:9).

Scripture demonstrates that salvation is an issue of the heart. It is not the words you say but the belief in your heart that leads to salvation. Salvation is the work of God in response to one's faith in Christ.

However, a natural overflow of believing in God is praying to Him. And what better moment to pray to Him than in the moment you realize the depth of your sin and your need for a Savior? Praying with your child in response to the gospel is a sincere conversation between a repentant sinner and a gracious God, not a spoken script to receive salvation. However, you could lead them in a prayer that goes something like this:

God, I've sinned against You, and I know that I can never make this right on my own. I trust that Jesus's sacrifice was enough to bring me into a real, life-changing relationship with You. Redeem my life, Lord. I cannot do it apart from You. I am making the choice to walk with You in my mind, heart, and actions every day, and I want to start today. Amen.

There is nothing magical about these words. They simply communicate the admission of sin and belief in God's saving power. Salvation is an issue of the heart.

If your child chooses to repent of their sin and believe in Jesus, celebrate this wonderful moment with them! Tell them they have made an amazing decision, and they are now part of God's family!

Salvation is the work of God in response to one's faith in Christ.

Seeing Jesus in
GENESIS–DEUTERONOMY

Memory Verse

For the wages of sin is death,
but the gift of God is eternal life
in Christ Jesus our Lord.

ROMANS 6:23

The Bible is
ALL ABOUT JESUS

Let's imagine we are going to put a puzzle together. Pretend you are holding the box in your hands. Now, carefully take the lid off, and dump all of the pieces out in front of you. Wow, look at all of those puzzle pieces! Each one is unique. Some have straight edges, but most have bumps, bends, and curves. Some are bright and colorful, while others are plain and simple. A pile of pieces doesn't seem that exciting, but when the puzzle is put together, it is no longer a big mess of random pieces but one big, beautiful picture!

In some ways, the Bible is like a puzzle. It includes many small stories that together tell one big story. Each verse and chapter in the Bible is a small glimpse of the bigger picture. Puzzles have a picture on the box of what the pieces make when they are all put together. Does the Bible also tell us what its pieces make altogether? Yes, it does!

The Bible is all about Jesus. The first part of the Bible, the Old Testament, shows us why we all need Jesus, and the second part of the Bible, the New Testament, tells us what happened after Jesus arrived!

You may be wondering, *Who is Jesus?* That is a great question. Jesus is God's Son. This means Jesus is God. Jesus is unlike anyone you have ever known before. And even though He lives in heaven, He wants to be in a relationship with you. Yes, you! He wants you to know Him, talk to Him, and be His friend forever. The Bible tells us everything we need to know about how to be close to Jesus. We have so much to learn about Jesus together! But, for today, let's start with this one truth: *Jesus loves you.*

Discuss Together

+ Who do you think Jesus is?

+ What questions do you have about Jesus?

Pray Together

+ **THANK** God for giving us the Bible so we can learn about Him.

+ **ASK** God to help you see how the whole Bible is about Jesus.

Old Testament: The first half of the Bible that records God's rules, the history of His people, and His promises of Jesus

Jesus is
THE CREATOR

For the wages of sin is death, but the gift of God
is eternal life in Christ Jesus our Lord.

ROMANS 6:23

READ TOGETHER

Genesis 1:1, Genesis 2:7

SUMMARIZE TOGETHER

Share something you noticed in today's Scripture reading.

Close your eyes. Go on... really close them! What do you see? Nothing, right? Just darkness. That is what existed before God created the earth, the heavens, and the people. Absolutely nothing. Zilch. Nada. God created every single thing that we see, feel, touch, and taste. He made mud, rocks, trees, flowers, and bugs. He made cats, dogs, tigers, and porcupines. He made planets, stars, clouds, and all of the galaxies. Imagine how big and strong God must be if He could make all of that!

The most special thing God made was people. People have something that nothing else God created has. People were created in the image of God. An image is a reflection or picture of something else. When you look into a mirror, you see an image of yourself. God created people to reflect who He is and what He is like. He created people to be a picture of Him. And do you know what?

Every person who has ever lived has been created in God's image. It wasn't just the first people that God made to reflect Him—it was all people. Even you!

The Bible tells us that Jesus was with God when He created the earth. Jesus existed with God before the earth was made because Jesus is God. It is through Jesus that God created all things. Nothing has ever been created without Jesus. Jesus is life, and He gives life to all living things. We can already see how important Jesus is! He has always existed with God the Father. Jesus is God. And Jesus gives life to all created things.

Discuss Together

+ John 1:3 says, "All things were created through [Jesus], and apart from him not one thing was created that has been created." List some things Jesus created.

+ How strong and powerful do you think Jesus is if all things were created through Him?

Pray Together

+ **THANK** God for creating all things through Jesus.

+ **ASK** God to help you understand His strength and power.

Jesus is PERFECT

— PRACTICE THE MEMORY VERSE —

For the wages of sin is death, but the gift of God
is eternal life in Christ Jesus our Lord.

ROMANS 6:23

READ TOGETHER
Genesis 3:1–7

SUMMARIZE TOGETHER
Share something you noticed in today's Scripture reading.

When God made the first people, Adam and Eve, He gave them one
rule to follow. There was a tree called the Tree of Knowledge of Good
and Evil, and they were not to eat the fruit that grew on this tree. But,
wow, did it sure look delicious! One day, Eve was walking in the garden when a snake approached her and started talking. Now, I've never
seen a talking snake before, have you? No, of course, you haven't!

But this was no ordinary snake. He was actually Satan pretending to
be a snake. Satan used to be one of God's angels. But a long, long
time ago, before Adam and Eve were created, he decided he didn't
want to serve God anymore. And even worse, he decided he didn't
want people to serve God either. The snake was on a mission to make
Eve disobey what God said. He offered her a piece of fruit from the
Tree of Knowledge of Good and Evil, and he told her that God's rule
about the fruit was silly. He said that if she ate the fruit, nothing bad
would happen. In fact, Satan said good things would happen.

Eve now had a choice to make. Would she choose to believe God and trust what He said? Or would she believe the snake and disobey God? This big choice is one every single person has to make. Now, the snake isn't slithering around today, tempting people to eat forbidden fruit. But God does tell us how He wants us to live in the Bible, and we all have to choose whether or not we will obey what He has said. Only, no one has ever been able to perfectly keep God's rules. Every single person has sinned. Well, all of them, except one. Jesus lived a perfect life. He did everything right and never made a mistake. Jesus isn't like anyone else who has ever lived—Jesus is perfect!

Discuss Together

+ Can you remember a time when you had to choose between doing the right thing and the wrong thing? Was it easy or hard to do the right thing?

+ Jesus is always kind, fair, loving, and true. What do you think it is like to be in a relationship with Jesus, who *always* does the right thing?

Pray Together

+ **THANK** Jesus for always doing what is right.

+ **ASK** God to teach you to live the way He wants you to.

Satan: The enemy of God whose mission is to separate people from God for eternity

Jesus is
FORGIVING

— PRACTICE THE MEMORY VERSE —

For the wages of sin is death, but the gift of God
is eternal life in Christ Jesus our Lord.

ROMANS 6:23

READ TOGETHER
Genesis 3:22–24

SUMMARIZE TOGETHER
Share something you noticed in today's Scripture reading.

Adam and Eve had a decision to make. They had to decide whether God told them the truth about the Tree of Knowledge of Good and Evil or if the snake was telling the truth. God said if they ate the fruit, it would lead to death. The snake, Satan, said it would lead to life.

Sadly, Eve believed the snake, not God, and she took a bite. Then, Adam took a bite. As soon as they ate the fruit, everything changed. They quickly found out it wasn't God who lied but the snake. They felt ashamed, scared, and sad about what they had done. Adam and Eve had disobeyed God—they had sinned. Instead of trusting God, they had trusted the snake. The fruit might have tasted good, but it came with consequences. Sin often has consequences in our lives, too.

Adam and Eve's consequence was they would have to live somewhere else now. God sent them away from the beautiful garden. He sent them away from Him. Now, they lived alone in a desert. What a very bad decision they had made. Their mistake meant nothing was as it was supposed to be.

Had Adam and Eve ruined everything? It may seem that way, but God knew they would sin before He even created them. In fact, God knows that all people, even you and me, will sin. And He has a plan to take care of the sins of people. One day, God would save people from their sin and get rid of the snake—Satan—once and for all because He loves people and does not want them to be separated from Him because of their sin. All along, the plan was not for people to be perfect but for Jesus to come to save imperfect people from their sin.

Jesus offers forgiveness to every sinner who will believe in Him. He offers to take the consequences of sin for Adam, Eve, you, me, and everyone so that even sinners can live with God, just as if they never sinned. Jesus is forgiving!

Jesus offers forgiveness to every sinner who will believe in Him.

Discuss Together

+ Let's imagine you disobeyed a rule at home and received a consequence. How would you feel if a friend or sibling offered to take your consequence for you?

+ Adam and Eve's sins brought consequences, but they could not stop God's plan. What does this tell you about God?

Pray Together

+ **THANK** God for sending Jesus to forgive your sins.

+ **ASK** God to help you understand the forgiveness He offers.

Sin: Thoughts, actions, and beliefs that go against the rules and ways of God

"

Jesus is
FORGIVING

"

Jesus is
STRONGER THAN SIN

For the wages of sin is death, but the gift of God
is eternal life in Christ Jesus our Lord.

ROMANS 6:23

READ TOGETHER
Genesis 4:3-7

SUMMARIZE TOGETHER
Share something you noticed in today's Scripture reading.

Adam and Eve had two sons, Cain and Abel. Abel was big and strong. He liked to hunt, fish, and sleep under the stars at night. Cain liked to grow fruits and vegetables. He spent his days working in his garden. One day, both Cain and Abel brought an offering to God to show Him they loved Him. Abel brought an animal, and Cain brought some vegetables. God accepted Abel's offering but told Cain his offering was not good. Cain was angry. He was very angry. Why did God not like what he brought Him? Was his offering bad? Was God being unfair to him? Cain thought God was playing favorites, choosing to accept Abel's offering and not his. But this was not the case.

It wasn't about playing favorites. It wasn't about God loving animals more than vegetables. It was about Cain and Abel's hearts. Abel brought his offering to God with a pure heart. He really loved God and wanted to share with Him something wonderful He had grown. Cain's heart was not the same. He wanted to show he was big and important and worthy of God's love. He wanted God to love him best. When God rejected Cain's offering, it showed the truth about Cain's heart. He was only thinking about himself and not about God.

God warned Cain to be careful, pay attention to his heart, and bring another offering that really was about loving and worshiping God. Cain said, "No." And then Cain did the very worst possible thing—he found Abel and ended his life. Cain wanted God to love him. He wanted things to be right between God and him. But he went about it all wrong. So horribly, terribly wrong.

Cain had sin in his heart. He was proud and hateful and did not listen to God. God could have helped him overcome his desire to sin. But instead, Cain let sin control him. God knew all people, not just Cain, would struggle with sin. And He knew that all sin would eventually lead to death. That is why one day, God would send Jesus, who would overcome sin and death and give eternal life to all who believe in Him. Jesus is stronger than sin!

God would send Jesus, who would overcome sin and death and give eternal life to all who believe in Him.

Discuss Together

+ What kind of offering was God looking for from Cain and Abel? Was it about what they gave or how they gave it?

+ Was Cain able to make things right between God and him on his own? Can we make things right between God and us on our own?

Pray Together

+ **THANK** God for sending Jesus through whom we overcome sin.

+ **ASK** God to teach you to live the way He wants you to.

Eternal Life: Living forever in God's presence without end

"

Jesus is
STRONGER
THAN SIN!

"

Jesus is the
SAVIOR OF THE WORLD

For the wages of sin is death, but the gift of God
is eternal life in Christ Jesus our Lord.

ROMANS 6:23

READ TOGETHER
Genesis 6:9–14

SUMMARIZE TOGETHER
Share something you noticed in today's Scripture reading.

Sin sure was a big problem for Adam and Eve and their sons, Cain
and Abel. And as more people were born and more families grew,
it became a really big, hairy, sticky, awful problem. Eventually, the
whole earth was full of people who only wanted to sin. They had
forgotten God altogether. They loved to do the wrong things. God
looked at the earth He created so carefully and saw how people
were treating it so recklessly. And He was sad. He wished people
had chosen to love and follow Him.

One man still loved God and did what He asked, though. His name
was Noah. God decided that all the people who refused to follow
His ways needed to be punished. He was going to send a flood—a
giant, torrential, colossal flood! Everyone would die except Noah
and his family and a big boat full of animals. God told Noah His
plan, and even though it seemed crazy, Noah listened. Noah built

the biggest boat anyone had ever seen and said it was for the day a big flood came. Everyone laughed. A flood? From where? They weren't even used to seeing rain where they lived!

Noah was right to trust God because a flood did come. Noah, his family, and a lot of smelly animals were safe on the ark. But everyone else was not safe and could not survive the flood. It rained and rained and rained, all day and all night. Until one day, it stopped. The whole earth was covered with deep, deep water. Noah's boat had nowhere to land. He waited until the water dried up, and when the boat finally rested on dry ground again, he opened the doors and stepped out.

The earth was empty like it had been when Adam and Eve were first created. God gave Noah and his family the same instructions He gave Adam and Eve: rule the earth, and have big families!

Then God gave Noah a promise. God promised that although sin would once again grow to cover the earth, He would not destroy the whole earth ever again. Instead, God would send someone, a Savior, who would destroy sin forever. Jesus is the Savior of the world!

God would send someone, a Savior, who would destroy sin forever.

Discuss Together

+ What was the consequence that all people of the earth (except Noah and his family) experienced for their sin?

+ Romans 6:23 says, "For the wages of sin is death, but the gift of God is eternal life in Christ Jesus our Lord." According to this verse, what does God give in place of the consequence of death?

Pray Together

+ **THANK** God that Jesus rescues us from our sin like the boat rescued Noah from the flood.

+ **ASK** God to help you trust Him, even when other people do not.

Salvation: The rescuing of sinners from sin

"

Jesus is

THE SAVIOR OF THE WORLD!

"

Jesus is the
ONLY WAY TO GOD

— PRACTICE THE MEMORY VERSE —

For the wages of sin is death, but the gift of God
is eternal life in Christ Jesus our Lord.

ROMANS 6:23

READ TOGETHER

Genesis 11:1–9

SUMMARIZE TOGETHER

Share something you noticed in today's Scripture reading.

After the flood, God told Noah and his family to fill the earth, to spread out and make homes for themselves all over the place. But as time passed and families grew, they decided they did not want to spread out anymore. Instead, they wondered if they could make a city to live in together and build a great, tall tower. They talked amongst themselves and decided that this was a good plan. They were smart and really strong, and they could build an amazingly tall tower if they all worked together. The tower would be so impressive it would make them famous! So, they started to build brick by brick. The tower grew taller, higher, and mightier every day. People would walk by the tower and admire how awesome it truly was. They were so impressed with themselves, and they probably believed God was impressed with their efforts, too.

But God was not impressed with His people. He had not told them to build a tower. The people wanted to be famous and important. God wanted them to listen to and obey Him. Being in a relationship with God is not about showing Him how smart or strong you are; it is about believing that God is the big, strong, and smart one and that He wants to come close to you.

God needed to stop them from building that tall but useless tower. So, He came down to the earth. He confused the people by making them all speak different languages and spread them out all over the face of the earth. He couldn't let them keep spending all their energy doing silly things like trying to prove they were the biggest and best. Instead, He wanted them to simply love and obey Him. As people, we can never get to God on our own because our sin separates us from God. If we want to be close to God, we don't need to build a tower or do anything big and impressive—we need to be forgiven of our sin. Jesus forgives the sins of all those who believe in Him. Jesus is the only way to God!

Jesus forgives the sins of all those who believe in Him.

Discuss Together

+ Building a tower was not the way to get to God. In John 14:6, Jesus says, "I am the way, the truth, and the life. No one comes to the Father except through me." What do you think is the way to get to God?

+ Do you ever feel like you need to be a good, strong, or smart person for God to love you? What does this story tell you about how to be close to God?

Pray Together

+ **THANK** God that we don't have to find a way to get to Him because He sent Jesus to us.

+ **ASK** God to help you know that He loves you even when you make mistakes.

"

Jesus is
THE ONLY
WAY TO GOD!

"

Jesus is a
PROMISE KEPT

— PRACTICE THE MEMORY VERSE —

For the wages of sin is death, but the gift of God
is eternal life in Christ Jesus our Lord.

ROMANS 6:23

READ TOGETHER

Genesis 17:1–8

SUMMARIZE TOGETHER

Share something you noticed in today's Scripture reading.

Have you ever heard God speak to you out loud? Most of us haven't. But there was a man in the Bible named Abram who did! Abram lived in a town called Haran, but God wanted Abram and his wife, Sarai, to trust Him and move to a new place. God did not tell Abram where He wanted him to go—He just told him to pack up and leave. He told Abram why, though, explaining that He was calling him to a new place, far away from his family and friends, to bless him and the whole world through him.

Abram believed God, and he obeyed God. But He did have one very big question. God wanted to bless the world through Abram and his family, but Abram did not have any children. His family was so small—only him and his wife, Sarai. And Abram and Sarai were in their nineties! They were too old to have a baby. How would God use their small, humble family? God told Abram his family would grow to number as many as the stars in the sky. He even changed Abram's name to Abraham to show that He was going to do something new and wonderful in Abram's life. God promised to give Abraham a son. And He promised to be with Abraham, to help him, protect him, and lead him. Although it took a long, long time, Abraham did have a son, and his son's name was Isaac. God was keeping His promises!

God chose Abraham's family for a very special purpose. One day, many hundreds of years later, another miracle Son would be born in Abraham's family, and His name would be Jesus. This family would one day be the family that the Savior of the world would come from. God would save the world from sin through Abraham's family. Jesus is the way God kept His promise to Abraham!

> God would save the world from sin through Abraham's family.

Discuss Together

+ God chose Abraham and Sarah, who were old and didn't have any children, as His special family. It seemed impossible for them to have a big family! Why do you think God chose them?

+ Abraham had to wait a long time, about twenty years, for God's promise of a son. Second Peter 3:9 says, "The Lord does not delay his promise, as some understand delay, but is patient with you, not wanting any to perish but all to come to repentance." What does this verse tell us about God not being slow?

Pray Together

+ **THANK** God that He kept His promise to Abraham.

+ **ASK** God to help you be patient when His plans feel slow.

"

Jesus is the way
GOD KEPT
HIS PROMISE
TO ABRAHAM!

"

Jesus is the
BETTER JOSEPH

For the wages of sin is death, but the gift of God
is eternal life in Christ Jesus our Lord.

ROMANS 6:23

READ TOGETHER
Genesis 50:17–21

SUMMARIZE TOGETHER
Share something you noticed in today's Scripture reading.

Abraham's son Isaac had a son named Jacob. Jacob had a son named Joseph. Well, actually, Jacob had a lot of sons—twelve to be exact! But Jacob liked Joseph best. He gave Joseph special gifts and treated him differently than his brothers. This made Joseph's brothers upset. They decided to get rid of Joseph. Now, this was a terrible plan that was not fair to Joseph. But God was not going to forget His promises to this special family. He was going to make good things come of this very bad plan.

Joseph's brothers sold him as a slave, and he ended up far from home in Egypt, where he served an Egyptian officer named Potiphar. Joseph worked hard, and Potiphar liked that! But then Potiphar's wife blamed Joseph for something he did not do, and he was thrown in jail. Now Joseph was away from his family, far from home, and in jail. How awful! Yet God helped Joseph get out of jail in an amazing way. And

Pharaoh, who was the leader of all of Egypt, asked Joseph to help the whole country survive a coming famine.

Joseph took care of the whole nation of Egypt, and he even took care of his brothers and family, who came to Egypt when they ran out of food. When Joseph's story seemed terribly bad, God used it for good. If Joseph's brothers had not sold him into slavery, he would not have been able to help feed so many people during the famine.

God used Joseph, who was treated unfairly, to save many people's lives. Joseph reminds us of Jesus. Jesus lived a perfect life, yet people accused Him of sinning and even put Him to death because they believed His sins were so bad. Even though it was unfair, Jesus willingly died so that His death could pay the price of other people's sins. Jesus died an unfair death so that all who believe in Him could have eternal life. Jesus is the better Joseph.

When Joseph's story seemed terribly bad, God used it for good.

Discuss Together

+ Even though God's special family made lots of mistakes, God was faithful to them. What mistakes did Joseph's brothers make? How did God use it for good?

+ People who love and serve God experience hard things sometimes. Second Corinthians 4:17–18 says, "For our momentary light affliction is producing for us an absolutely incomparable eternal weight of glory. So we do not focus on what is seen, but on what is unseen. For what is seen is temporary, but what is unseen is eternal." How do these verses describe the hard things we experience now? How do they describe what those who believe will experience in eternity with Jesus?

Pray Together

+ **THANK** God that He can use all things for good, even when they seem bad.

+ **ASK** God to help you look forward to eternity with Jesus.

"

JESUS DIED AN UNFAIR DEATH SO THAT ALL WHO BELIEVE IN HIM COULD HAVE *eternal life.*

"

Jesus is
THE RESCUER

For the wages of sin is death, but the gift of God
is eternal life in Christ Jesus our Lord.

ROMANS 6:23

READ TOGETHER
Exodus 2:2–6, 23–25

SUMMARIZE TOGETHER
Share something you noticed in today's Scripture reading.

God's chosen people—the family of Abraham, Isaac, Jacob, and Joseph—lived in Egypt for a long time. They were a people group called the Hebrews. But things didn't go very well for the Hebrews in Egypt. The Egyptians enslaved the Hebrews. They made them work long hours in the hot sun, and they punished them if they stopped working. The Hebrews longed to be free, to be able to play and laugh and enjoy life. Pharaoh even said that all Hebrew baby boys must be thrown into the river. He was very cruel to God's people, the Hebrews.

One Hebrew mother had a baby boy and did not want him to be taken away, so she hid him from those who wanted to take him until she couldn't anymore. Then, she placed him in a basket and set him in the river. She hoped he would be okay and sent her daughter to watch what happened next. Pharaoh's daughter found the baby in the river, and she adopted him as her own son.

He was named Moses and grew up in the palace as one of Pharaoh's family. Moses knew he was not an Egyptian but a Hebrew. He didn't like the way the Egyptians treated the Hebrew people. One day, Moses saw an Egyptian hurting a Hebrew, and likely out of anger, Moses killed the Egyptian. He should not have done this. Pharaoh was very mad at Moses. Moses ran away to the desert and lived far from Pharaoh and the Hebrew slaves. There, he got married, had a family, and became a shepherd.

Moses had a new life in the desert far away from Egypt. But God was with His people in Egypt. He heard their prayers for God to save them. And He was going to use Moses to answer those prayers and lead the Hebrews to freedom. There was another person God sent to answer the prayer of His people a long time later. That person was Jesus. Just as God sent Moses to rescue the Hebrews from Egypt, God sent Jesus to rescue all who believe in Him from sin and death. Jesus is the rescuer!

God sent Jesus to rescue all who believe in Him from sin and death.

Discuss Together

+ Exodus 2:25 says, "God saw the Israelites, and God knew." What does this verse tell you about God and how He cares for His people?

+ Pharaoh tried to kill Moses, but God protected his life. What does this tell you about God?

Pray Together

+ **THANK** God for being near and hearing His people when they are going through hard times.

+ **ASK** God to be near you and help you if you face something hard.

"

Jesus is
THE RESCUER!

"

JESUS IS THE RESCUER / 53

Jesus is the
TRUE PASSOVER LAMB

— PRACTICE THE MEMORY VERSE —

For the wages of sin is death, but the gift of God
is eternal life in Christ Jesus our Lord.

ROMANS 6:23

READ TOGETHER

Exodus 6:2–8

SUMMARIZE TOGETHER

Share something you noticed in today's Scripture reading.

One day, Moses was tending to his sheep in the desert when he saw something that startled him. It was a bush that was on fire. Yet the leaves were not burning, and the fire was not affecting the bush at all. Moses could not believe his eyes! When he went to get a closer look, God talked to Moses right from the middle of that burning bush! God told Moses He had heard the prayers of the Hebrews. God was going to lead them to freedom, and Moses was going to help.

God chose Moses to deliver His people from slavery to freedom, but Moses didn't think he was the man for the job. God told Moses He would be with him and to trust Him. So, Moses did what God asked and approached Pharaoh to say, "Let my people go!" Pharaoh said, "No." Moses wasn't sure what to do next, but God knew. God sent plagues of darkness, flies, frogs, and locusts to show Pharaoh how strong He was and get him to free the Hebrews. Pharaoh still refused. So, God sent one last plague, and it was the worst one yet. The oldest son of every house would die in this plague. Thankfully, God also made a way to be saved from this plague. If anyone brushed the blood of a pure and spotless lamb on their doorposts, the angel of death would pass right over their home, and no one inside would die.

Many people died on the night of this plague, which is now called the Passover. But no one who had the blood of a spotless lamb on their door frame died. Pharaoh's son died, and Pharaoh was very sad. After this, Pharaoh finally agreed to let the Hebrews go. Moses led the people away from Egypt and into freedom. Like the lamb killed for the Passover, Jesus was pure and sinless, yet He died. And His blood covers all who believe in Him, just as the lamb's blood protected those who put it on their door frames. Those who believe in Jesus are safe from death and are given eternal life by the blood of Jesus. Jesus is the true Passover Lamb!

> Those who believe in Jesus are safe from death and are given eternal life.

Discuss Together

+ How did God protect His people from the final plague?

+ Read Exodus 15:2–3 below.

   The Lord is my strength and my song;
   he has become my salvation.
   This is my God, and I will praise him,
   my father's God, and I will exalt him.
   The Lord is a warrior;
   the Lord is his name.

   These verses were part of a song the Hebrews sang to God to thank Him for delivering them from Egypt. How did the Hebrews describe God in these verses?

Pray Together

+ **THANK** Jesus for shedding His blood to protect you.

+ **ASK** God to help you trust His plan as Moses did.

"

Jesus is
THE TRUE PASSOVER LAMB!

"

Jesus is the
KEEPER OF GOD'S COMMANDS

— PRACTICE THE MEMORY VERSE —

For the wages of sin is death, but the gift of God
is eternal life in Christ Jesus our Lord.

ROMANS 6:23

READ TOGETHER
Exodus 20:1–3

SUMMARIZE TOGETHER
Share something you noticed in today's Scripture reading.

Now that God's people were free from Egypt, everything was going to be great, right? The Hebrews were now a new nation called Israel. The Israelites thought God would lead them to their new home right away. They called their new home the Promised Land because it was the land God promised to them. But God didn't lead them straight there. Instead, He led them on a long journey in a hot, dry, dusty desert. They lived in tents and sometimes had a hard time finding food. But God was taking care of them. He provided quail to hunt and manna (which was a special kind of bread that came from heaven) to feed them.

God also took care of them in another way by giving them some rules to follow. God wanted His people, the Israelites, to live differently from other people. The Israelites were to respect and care for each other and not lie or steal. And they were especially not to worship other gods. Their God was the one true God. Anyone else who claimed to be a god was just not telling the truth. God promised that if His people loved Him and followed His rules, they would be blessed. God told them to keep His commands no matter what. Do you think the Israelites listened? Well, they might have tried to, but they couldn't keep all the rules.

The people of God walked away from God, even though He had been so faithful to them. God gave His people a consequence for their disobedience. They had to wait to enter the Promised Land. They would wait in the desert, living in tents because they refused to listen to God. Even though the people didn't trust God, God still loved them. He never gave up on them. And His plan to save the world from sin had not been stopped because it didn't depend on how well people obeyed Him. It all depended on Jesus. Jesus is the One who perfectly kept all God's rules. Through Jesus's obedience, God offers salvation from sin to all who believe.

Even though the people didn't trust God, God still loved them. He never gave up on them.

Discuss Together

+ When the people chose not to follow the rules, did it ruin God's plan? Why or why not?

+ The Israelites were disobedient, yet God did not give up on them. Why do you think God stayed with and continued to provide for the Israelites?

Pray Together

+ **THANK** God that His plan to save us from our sin does not depend on how well we follow His rules.

+ **ASK** God to help you obey Him because you love Him and His rules are good.

"

Jesus is
THE ONE
WHO PERFECTLY
KEPT ALL
GOD'S RULES.

"

Jesus is
THE PERFECT SACRIFICE

— **PRACTICE THE MEMORY VERSE** —

For the wages of sin is death, but the gift of God
is eternal life in Christ Jesus our Lord.

ROMANS 6:23

READ TOGETHER
Exodus 40:33–38

SUMMARIZE TOGETHER
Share something you noticed in today's Scripture reading.

Do you know what made the Israelites so special? They were God's chosen people. In the beginning, God dwelled with Adam and Eve until they sinned and had to leave the garden. Now, God had chosen a special group of people to live with again. God didn't walk and talk with the people, but His presence lived with them. He even had them build a special box, called the ark of the covenant, upon which His presence could rest. And then He told them to build a wonderful and beautiful tent to put the ark of the covenant inside.

This tent was called the tabernacle. The tabernacle was where people came to meet with God. But, before they could meet with God, they needed to be sure they were ready. God cannot be in the presence of sin, remember? So those who met with Him had to be cleansed from their sin. They did this by shedding an animal's blood. There were priests who would take the animal's blood and sprinkle it on the altar inside the tabernacle. The death of the animal paid the price for the people's sins. But the problem was that people sinned every day. They sinned all the time. They kept having to offer animals as a sacrifice for their sins, day after day after day. And even when they were right with God, they could not just go into His presence and talk to Him. Only the priests could do that. And even the priests could only enter God's presence once per year.

So God was with His people, yet they still were not as close to Him as they wanted to be. But this wasn't the end of the story. God would make a way for His people to be close to Him all the time. He would send Jesus, the perfect sacrifice, whose blood would pay for all the people's sins. Jesus only had to give His life one time. Jesus is God, and He is a man. Jesus is also sinless. Jesus was the perfect sacrifice, and through Him, all people can come into a close and personal relationship with God.

> Jesus was the perfect sacrifice, and through Him, all people can come into a close and personal relationship with God.

Discuss Together

+ God's plan was always to live with His people. What kept God's people from being close to Him?

+ Hebrews 7:27 says, "[Jesus] doesn't need to offer sacrifices every day, as high priests do—first for their own sins, then for those of the people. He did this once for all time when he offered himself." According to this verse, how is Jesus's sacrifice different from the sacrifices that the priest offered in the tabernacle?

Pray Together

Grown-ups: this may be a good time to reference *Sharing the Good News of the Gospel with Children* on page 16–17.

+ **THANK** Jesus for sacrificing His life to pay for all the sins of all people.

+ **ASK** God to forgive you for your sins because Jesus has paid the price for them.

Sacrifice: An animal or object given to God to pay the price for sin

"

GOD WOULD
make a way
FOR HIS PEOPLE
TO BE CLOSE
TO HIM
all the time.

"

Seeing Jesus in
JOSHUA-MALACHI

Memory Verse

For the word of the Lord is right,

and all his work is trustworthy.

PSALM 33:4

Jesus is
FAITHFUL

— PRACTICE THE MEMORY VERSE —

For the word of the Lord is right, and all
his work is trustworthy.

PSALM 33:4

READ TOGETHER
Joshua 1:5–7

SUMMARIZE TOGETHER
Share something you noticed in today's Scripture reading.

After forty years of wandering and waiting in the desert, God finally
said it was time for His people to enter the land He promised them.
They had a new leader, Joshua, and God was leading them into a
new land. But there was a BIG problem. The land God gave them
already belonged to someone else, the Canaanites. The Canaanites
were mean, hated God, and were really strong. When God's people
saw the Canaanites, they were scared! And they began to doubt
that God was powerful enough to take this land from the Canaanites and give it to them.

God told them not to fear. The Canaanites were big and mean, but
He had a plan. God led the Israelite soldiers toward the Promised
Land and the city of Jericho. He showed them how mighty and
strong He was by parting another sea for them to walk through, just
like He parted the Red Sea when Moses led them out of Egypt.

Finally, when they saw Jericho and approached the tall walls surrounding it, God told them what to do. Instead of drawing their swords and charging forward, God told them to walk around the walls. The Israelites might have been thinking, *What? Walk? What good is that going to do?* It didn't make any sense! The Israelites didn't understand, but they did obey.

For seven days, they walked around the walls. And on the seventh day, God told them to shout as loud as possible. When they shouted, the city's walls came tumbling down, and they defeated the strong Canaanites like it was nothing. The Israelites couldn't believe it! God was keeping His promises! After all their waiting, doubting, and fear, they were finally going to live in the Promised Land.

Every time we see God keep His promises in the Bible, it's a reminder that He is always faithful and always does what He says He will do. Jesus is faithful to be our Savior, Redeemer, Deliverer, Life, and Hope. Every story we read in the Bible is true, and everything the Bible teaches us about Jesus is true. Jesus always has been and always will be faithful!

> Every time we see God keep His promises in the Bible, it's a reminder that He is always faithful.

Discuss Together

+ Did you think walking around the walls of Jericho would make the walls fall down? Why do you think God helped the Israelites conquer the Promised Land in this way?

+ Read today's Bible reading, Joshua 1:5–7, again. Why do you think God told the Israelites to be strong and courageous?

Pray Together

+ **THANK** Jesus for always being faithful.

+ **ASK** God to help you be strong and courageous as you trust in Him.

"

JESUS ALWAYS HAS BEEN AND ALWAYS WILL BE

faithful!

"

Jesus is
THE KING

— PRACTICE THE MEMORY VERSE —

For the word of the Lord is right, and all
his work is trustworthy.

PSALM 33:4

READ TOGETHER
Judges 2:1–2, Judges 17:6

SUMMARIZE TOGETHER
Share something you noticed in today's Scripture reading.

The Promised Land was everything God said it would be. It was the perfect place for God's people to live and grow their families. Joshua told all of the Israelites to follow God and obey His rules. If they did so, God would bless them in the Promised Land. But the Israelites chose not to do this. Instead, they did the same things as the people around them who didn't love God or know His ways. They started worshiping other gods, who were not really gods but just silly little statues. The Israelites disobeyed and sinned instead of living as God told them to. They chose to believe that sin was better than God, just like Adam and Eve did.

This led to many, many consequences. So God put leaders in place to help the Israelites follow His commands. Israel's leaders were called judges. At first, the judges tried to follow God and show the rest of the nation how to follow God. But, as time went on, the judges became worse and worse and more and more sinful. However, something incredible happened. Even with these sinful judges, God showed up. God sometimes sent His Spirit to help the judges and save His people. This wasn't because the judges were good—it was because God is faithful. Even when people fail, God keeps His word. He promised to be with His people, so He was.

Even more than this, God saw that His people needed a King. They needed someone who would lead them to Him and away from sin. God knew His people struggled with sin and needed a Savior. This was a sad chapter for God's people, but redemption was coming. God would send Jesus to be their King, forgive their sin, and show them how to obey His ways. God was faithful to the Israelites in the time of the judges, and He would be faithful to send Jesus, too.

Discuss Together

+ When God's people sin, does He abandon them?

+ What do you think redemption means?

Pray Together

+ **THANK** God for being faithful.

+ **ASK** God to help you obey His ways.

Jesus is
THE REDEEMER

— PRACTICE THE MEMORY VERSE —

For the word of the Lord is right, and all
his work is trustworthy.

PSALM 33:4

READ TOGETHER
Ruth 4:14–15

SUMMARIZE TOGETHER
Share something you noticed in today's Scripture reading.

When the judges ruled Israel, there was a family with a husband and wife and two sons who moved away from Israel to a place called Moab. They moved because life in Israel was hard, and they were running out of food. While in Moab, the two sons married Moabite women named Ruth and Orpah. But then, the two sons and their father died. Suddenly, Naomi, the mother of the sons, and Ruth and Orpah, their wives, were all alone. They were all so sad. Naomi and Ruth decided to move back to Israel, but Orpah stayed in Moab. It seems like Ruth should have stayed in Moab, as well, because that's where her family lived, but instead, Ruth chose to go with Naomi so she could help her.

In Israel, Ruth worked hard to find food for her and Naomi. One day, she was gathering grain in fields that belonged to a man named Boaz. Boaz was a nice man. He helped Ruth and Naomi because he knew they were hungry and had no family. In fact, Boaz was not just nice, but he was also a distant family member of Naomi, which meant that he could marry Ruth according to the Law. Boaz's kindness in sharing his food was helpful, but the women wanted more than this. They wanted a home to live in and someone to protect and provide for them. Ruth decided to ask Boaz if he would marry her, take care of Naomi, and restore their happiness. Boaz said, "Yes"! He married Ruth and took care of Naomi like she was his very own mother. Boaz and Ruth had a baby boy, and the whole family was overjoyed! They praised God for giving them so much joy after all the sadness they experienced.

Boaz was a wonderful redeemer for Naomi and Ruth, but he was just a picture of a better Redeemer—Jesus! Jesus redeems those who believe in Him from their sin. He gives joy for sadness and hope in the place of pain. Jesus is the Redeemer of the whole world. He can make all things new!

Boaz was a wonderful redeemer for Naomi and Ruth, but he was just a picture of a better Redeemer—Jesus!

Discuss Together

+ How do you think Naomi and Ruth felt when Boaz agreed to care for them and be their family?

+ Read Psalm 103:3–5 below.

He forgives all your iniquity;
he heals all your diseases.
He redeems your life from the Pit;
he crowns you with faithful love and compassion.
He satisfies you with good things;
your youth is renewed like the eagle.

What do you think the term "redeem" means? How do these verses describe some of the things God does when He redeems His people?

Pray Together

+ **THANK** God that He redeems people.

+ **ASK** God to redeem any sadness or pain in your life.

Redeem: To buy one's freedom

"

JESUS IS THE REDEEMER OF THE WHOLE WORLD. HE CAN MAKE

all things new!

"

Jesus is
THE BETTER DAVID

— PRACTICE THE MEMORY VERSE —

For the word of the Lord is right, and all
his work is trustworthy.

PSALM 33:4

READ TOGETHER
1 Chronicles 17:7–10

SUMMARIZE TOGETHER
Share something you noticed in today's Scripture reading.

God's people waited a long time to enter the Promised Land, and you would have thought they would have never stopped praising God once they finally got to live there. But, as it is for all people, sin was a problem for the Israelites. The priests, people who were supposed to lead them in worshiping God, were leading people away from God instead of toward Him. They loved themselves more than they loved God.

God told His people He would be the King of their nation, but the further the people got from God, the more they wanted a human, not God, as their king. God gave them what they wanted, even though He knew it wasn't what was best for them.

The first king was named Saul. Saul turned his back on God and was not a good king. So God promised to give them a new king who would love and follow Him. This second king was David. Not many people thought David would be a good king. He was only a little kid who watched after sheep! He wasn't big, strong, or impressive. But David trusted God. And that is why God chose him.

When David was young, he defeated one of Israel's greatest enemies, a Philistine named Goliath, with God's help. Later, once David became king, he put God first and encouraged all of Israel to love and worship God. He brought the tabernacle (where God's presence lived) to a high hilltop in the center of Israel. He loved God and showed others how to love Him, too.

David led people to God, but he was still imperfect. He made lots of mistakes, and he experienced the consequences of his mistakes. David reminds us of another King—King Jesus. Jesus leads us to God and shows us how to worship God, like David. But, unlike King David, Jesus is perfect. He will reign forever over all the earth with wisdom, love, and truth. When we look at David's life, we see a good king. When we look at Jesus, we see a perfect King. Jesus is the better David.

Unlike King David, Jesus is perfect. He will reign forever over all the earth with wisdom, love, and truth.

Discuss Together

+ What good things did David do?

+ In what ways is Jesus a better king than David?

Pray Together

+ **THANK** God for including imperfect people in the big story of Scripture.

+ **ASK** God to help you lead others to worship Him as David did.

"

DAVID REMINDS US OF ANOTHER KING—

King Jesus.

"

Jesus is the
ANSWER TO
OUR PRAYERS

— PRACTICE THE MEMORY VERSE —

For the word of the Lord is right, and all
his work is trustworthy.

PSALM 33:4

READ TOGETHER
Psalm 9:1–3

SUMMARIZE TOGETHER
Share something you noticed in today's Scripture reading.

The Bible holds many amazing stories about the men and women God chose to be part of His plan to save the world from sin. Sometimes these people experienced difficult things, sometimes they made mistakes, and sometimes they struggled to do what God asked of them. We, too, might face these same things in our relationship with God. And when we do, we might wonder:

Can I tell God that I am having a hard time doing the right thing?

Should I ask God to hurry up and answer my prayer sooner?

When I make a big mistake, what should I say to God?

The book of Psalms answers all of these questions and more. Psalms show us how God's people throughout time have talked to God in their highs and lows, in the good and the bad, when they feel close to God, and when they feel He is far away. Some psalms express sadness, some show joy, and others are desperate pleas for God to help. There are psalms that are poems and psalms that are songs, but all psalms are prayers to God. The psalms help us see that we are invited to share our true feelings with God at all times. We can talk to Him when we are happy or hopeful and also when we are disappointed or angry.

Even though they were written hundreds of years before his birth, we can even see Jesus in the psalms. There are over sixty times when Jesus is referred to in the book of Psalms. There are psalms that predict from which family Jesus will be born (Psalm 89:3–4), that Jesus will be rejected by men (Psalm 118:22), that Jesus will calm a stormy sea (Psalm 107:28–29), and that Jesus will reign forever (Psalm 45:6–7). God's people prayed and spoke about Jesus, even before they knew His name. They didn't know when, but they knew a Savior and Redeemer was coming one day who would be the best answer to all of their prayers. And He is! Jesus is everything the writers of Psalms said He would be and more.

The psalms help us see that we are invited to share our true feelings with God at all times.

Discuss Together

+ Read Psalm 102:1–2 below. What do you think the author was feeling?

  Lord, hear my prayer;
  let my cry for help come before you.
  Do not hide your face from me in my day of trouble.
  Listen closely to me;
  answer me quickly when I call.

+ What emotions do you have that you might want to talk to God about?

Pray Together

+ **THANK** God for listening to our prayers.

+ **ASK** God for His help with the things going on in your life.

"

GOD'S PEOPLE PRAYED AND SPOKE ABOUT JESUS *even before* THEY KNEW HIS NAME.

"

Jesus is the
KING OF ALL KINGS

For the word of the Lord is right, and all
his work is trustworthy.

PSALM 33:4

READ TOGETHER
1 Kings 6:11–13

SUMMARIZE TOGETHER
Share something you noticed in today's Scripture reading.

Put your hand over your heart. Do you feel it beating? Ba-bum, ba-bum. In your physical body, your heart pumps blood and oxygen to every finger, toe, and cell. That thumping in your chest keeps your whole body healthy. The Bible tells us we have another kind of heart, too. We have a spiritual heart. Our spiritual heart helps us think, feel, and make decisions.

When David, the shepherd king, was very old, he died, and his son Solomon became king. Before David died, he told Solomon that if he loved and served God with his whole heart, then he would be a great and successful king. Solomon started out loving God. He built God a temple, a permanent place where He could live that was much more beautiful and glorious than the tabernacle tent God's presence lived in while David was king.

Even though Solomon built this big, beautiful home for God, his whole heart didn't belong to God. He started breaking some of God's rules because he thought maybe God's ways weren't the best ways. At first, Solomon only broke a couple of rules, but that led to him breaking more and more until he forgot about God's ways altogether and only did what He wanted.

It turns out that even though Solomon did big things for God by building Him a home to live in, Solomon wasn't the kind of king God wanted for his people. God wanted a king who loved Him with his whole heart, not a king who looked good on the outside but on the inside loved to disobey God.

God knew that no human king could ever be the kind of king He desired. That's why God's plan all along was to send Jesus, who would be the King of all kings. Jesus served God with His whole life, even when it meant He had to die on a cross. When He paid for all people's sins on the cross, Jesus made a way for God to live in the hearts of everyone who receives His forgiveness for their sins. Jesus was a better King who built a better home for God.

> **Jesus made a way for God to live in the hearts of everyone who receives His forgiveness for their sins.**

Discuss Together

+ What do you think it would look like for you to love God with your whole heart?

+ First John 1:9 says, "If we confess our sins, he is faithful and righteous to forgive us our sins and to cleanse us from all unrighteousness." What do these verses say we should do when we sin against God? And what does God do in response?

Pray Together

+ **THANK** Jesus for being the King of all kings.

+ **ASK** God to help you love Him with your whole heart.

"

GOD'S PLAN
all along
WAS TO SEND JESUS, WHO WOULD BE THE
King of all kings.

"

Jesus is the
GIVER OF NEW LIFE

— PRACTICE THE MEMORY VERSE —

For the word of the Lord is right, and all
his work is trustworthy.

PSALM 33:4

READ TOGETHER
1 Kings 18:21

SUMMARIZE TOGETHER
Share something you noticed in today's Scripture reading.

During and after King Solomon's reign, things went from bad to worse to the very worst. In fact, things got so bad that the entire nation of Israel split in two because they were fighting so much. Not only were God's people divided into two groups, but they were also worshiping other gods. These other gods were just statues and not even real! This wasn't what God wanted for His people. So He sent messengers called prophets to tell them to stop loving sin and start loving God. One of these messengers was named Elijah.

Elijah invited those who believed in one of the silly statue gods named Baal to a contest. Both Elijah and the Baal believers would pray to their gods and ask for fire to fall from heaven. Whichever one sent down fire would be known as the one true God. First, the prophets of Baal prayed. They prayed for a long time and said a lot of words. But nothing happened. No fire fell. Then, Elijah prayed to his God. And not a moment after the words left his lips, fire fell down from heaven in a raging blaze.

Everyone had gathered to watch this contest, and they were amazed! Elijah's God was truly powerful! But Baal had done nothing. He didn't answer or move or even hear. Because of this, everyone began worshiping the real God.

Sadly, not long after the fire, the people forgot God again. Even when God did big, amazing things, people didn't choose to serve Him. The problem wasn't that God hadn't done anything amazing for them. The problem was their hearts. Sin had broken their hearts and made it impossible for them to love God as they should. They needed new hearts—hearts that loved God and followed Him. One day, Jesus would come and give them new hearts in place of their old ones. Jesus would cause them to be born again into a new life with a new heart. Then, they could follow and love God. Without Jesus, no one can love God the way they should. Jesus is the giver of new life!

Without Jesus, no one can love
God the way they should.

Discuss Together

+ What happened when the Baal believers prayed to Baal? What happened when Elijah prayed to God? What does this tell you about God?

+ What do you think it means to be born again?

Pray Together

+ **THANK** God for giving new hearts to those who believe in Jesus.

+ **ASK** God to help you know that He is the one true God.

Born Again: Receiving a new spiritual life through Jesus's forgiveness of sins

"

Jesus is
THE GIVER
OF NEW LIFE!

"

Jesus is the
PROPHET, PRIEST, AND KING

— PRACTICE THE MEMORY VERSE —

For the word of the Lord is right, and all
his work is trustworthy.

PSALM 33:4

READ TOGETHER
2 Kings 17:22–23

SUMMARIZE TOGETHER
Share something you noticed in today's Scripture reading.

God is patient. He is very patient. But He is also just. "Just" means "to do what is right and fair." After Israel split into two, God warned His people for a long time that if they didn't stop sinning and start following Him, then there would be consequences. But God's people didn't listen. They only sinned more and more and more. And so, because He is just, the time came for God to give His people the consequences they deserved. God allowed His people to be conquered and taken away from their homes by nations bigger and stronger than them. The Israelites were exiled or sent away from home and lived as slaves in countries called Assyria and Babylon. Their sin cost them everything. They were brokenhearted.

The Israelites had done so many things wrong. Some of them believed God would find someone else to be His chosen people now.

But that's not what God was going to do. Instead, He said that although His people had been unfaithful, He would never be unfaithful to them. He was not going to leave them. No, He was committed to them and loved them, even though they had sinned so greatly. And He was going to restore and redeem them from their sin and all they had lost. He would send a new King who would also be a Prophet and Priest. This Prophet, Priest, and King would help God's people love God with their whole hearts. This King would be wise, just, and good. He would be the King they needed all along.

Even when God's people make mistakes, He does not give up on them. He sends them a Savior to redeem them, forgive them, and make their hearts new again. God would send Jesus to make right what people have made wrong. Jesus would restore what was broken and heal what was sick. He would be their Savior!

Discuss Together

+ What does today's devotion tell you about what God is like?

+ What do you think God's response to your sin is?

Pray Together

+ **THANK** God for always being faithful to you.

+ **ASK** God to help you be faithful to Him.

Jesus is
THE REBUILDER

For the word of the Lord is right, and all
his work is trustworthy.

PSALM 33:4

READ TOGETHER
Jeremiah 29:10–11, Nehemiah 2:17–18

SUMMARIZE TOGETHER
Share something you noticed in today's Scripture reading.

Do you have a space that feels special and safe? The Promised Land was that place for the Israelites. However, because the Israelites disobeyed God, they had to live far, far from their homes for seventy years. That's a long time! Finally, God made a way for them to return to Jerusalem from the places they had been sent. After a long journey, they arrived at what used to be their special place, but now it was a huge mess! All of the buildings and houses were falling down, and the temple, the place where God's presence lived, was totally ruined.

There were three men who led the Israelites in rebuilding their broken city. Their names were Zerubbabel, Ezra, and Nehemiah. For many years, these men worked to rebuild the city and temple. But, even more than that, they wanted to rebuild the Israelite people's commitment to loving and serving God. They did succeed in helping many people make their homes in Jerusalem. But they didn't succeed in convincing the people to love and serve God. The people kept ignoring God's rules and doing whatever they wanted instead.

Zerubbabel, Ezra, and Nehemiah knew God had promised that one day His people would return from exile to their homeland. And they knew God promised to give Israel a good future and hope. But God's people were a mess! They were making bad choices all over again. The problem was that the people didn't need a new city to live in; they needed new hearts. Their hearts loved to sin. They needed hearts that loved God more than sin. The Israelites needed Jesus. Only Jesus could truly rebuild the Israelites into the people God wanted them to be. Only He could change them from the inside out by forgiving their sin and giving them His Spirit to help them live in the way God wanted. Jesus is the true rebuilder of God's people, and though He had not arrived yet, He would come someday soon.

Discuss Together

+ What did God promise His people in Jeremiah 29:10–11? Did He fulfill this promise?

+ Could God's people live in the way God wanted them to on their own? Whose help did they need?

Pray Together

+ **THANK** Jesus for forgiving you when you don't live the way God desires.

+ **ASK** Jesus to help you live in the way God wants you to.

Jesus is
ALWAYS WORKING

— PRACTICE THE MEMORY VERSE —

For the word of the Lord is right, and all
his work is trustworthy.

PSALM 33:4

READ TOGETHER
Malachi 3:1

SUMMARIZE TOGETHER
Share something you noticed in today's Scripture reading.

Hooray! High fives! Cheers! We have explored the entire Old Testament! Through the Old Testament, we have clearly seen Jesus and our need for Him. And goodness, God's people surely need a Savior! Starting at the very beginning of the Old Testament with Adam and Eve and continuing until the very end when the Israelites were trying to rebuild Jerusalem, we have watched God's people choose sin over obeying God, time and time again.

Sin carries consequences, and God's people certainly experienced lots of consequences because God is just and always does what is right. But they also experienced God's grace. No matter how sinful the people were, God did not leave them or stop loving them. He never stopped caring for them, and He always fulfilled His promise to them.

One promise that He has not yet fulfilled at the end of the Old Testament is the promise to send the Savior, who is Jesus. The people were still watching and waiting. And unfortunately, they had a lot more waiting to do. After the very last verse of the Old Testament was written, it was four hundred years before the first words of the New Testament were written. It must have seemed like a really long wait. However, we learn in Galatians 4:4 that Jesus came at just the right time.

The waiting was hard. But Jesus was working, even in the waiting. And Jesus was with His people in the waiting, even if He wasn't yet physically walking the earth with them. Jesus is always working. He is always there—even when we can't see or hear Him. God's people had to trust this in the time between the Old and New Testaments, and we also need to trust this today. God is always right on time. We can trust His timing. And we can trust that Jesus is with us while we wait.

Through the Old Testament, we have clearly seen Jesus and our need for Him.

Discuss Together

+ What is one story in the Old Testament that helped you see Jesus?

+ What is one way the Old Testament taught you that everyone, including yourself, needs Jesus?

Pray Together

+ **THANK** God that He is always working.

+ **ASK** God to show you that He is there, even when you cannot see or hear Him.

"

JESUS IS
always working.
HE IS ALWAYS THERE—EVEN WHEN WE CAN'T SEE OR HEAR HIM.

"

Seeing Jesus in
MATTHEW–JOHN

Memory Verse

For everyone who calls on the
name of the Lord will be saved.

ROMANS 10:13

Jesus is
IMMANUEL

— PRACTICE THE MEMORY VERSE —

For everyone who calls on
the name of the Lord will be saved.

ROMANS 10:13

READ TOGETHER
Matthew 1:21–23

SUMMARIZE TOGETHER
Share something you noticed in today's Scripture reading.

What is something that you had to wait a really long time for? How did you feel when you finally received the thing you had to wait for? Today, we will begin to look at the New Testament, and we will finally see the arrival of Jesus! Think of all of the people who were waiting and hoping for the Savior to be born in the Old Testament. There were so many! Think of all the times God reminded His people that He was going to send them a King, Prophet, and Priest. This Savior would serve God's people, teach them to love, and free them from their sin. Now, finally, all of those hopes and promises are going to come true in Jesus!

Jesus was born as a baby—a very special baby. God chose Mary to be Jesus's mother, and the Holy Spirit caused Jesus to grow in Mary's belly. An angel came to Mary to explain all of this, and Mary believed the angel and agreed to raise Jesus as her son. Jesus is the only person who has ever been born this way. That's because Jesus is both man and God! Mary's husband was named Joseph. An angel appeared to Joseph, as well, and explained to him that Mary was going to have a very special baby. The angel told Joseph the baby's name would be Jesus and that He would be called Immanuel.

"Jesus" means "God saves," and "Immanuel" means "God with us." Through Jesus, God was going to offer all people salvation from their sins. God also sent Jesus down to earth to be with people. He was a child just like you. He had birthdays, He got sick, He spent time with His friends and family, and He experienced good things and bad things in life. Jesus is God with us; He is Immanuel. He came to us to save us. Isn't that amazing? Jesus could have stayed far away in heaven, but He didn't. Jesus is the Savior God promised. Jesus is Immanuel!

> Through Jesus, God was going to offer all people salvation from their sins.

Discuss Together

+ Matthew 28:20b says, "And remember, I am with you always, to the end of the age." According to this verse, is Jesus still with us today?

+ What does it mean to you that Jesus is with you?

Pray Together

+ **THANK** Jesus for coming to earth to be with us and save us from our sin.

+ **ASK** Jesus to help you understand that He is always with you.

New Testament: The second half of the Bible that records the life, ministry, death, and resurrection of Jesus, as well as what happened after He returned to heaven

"

JESUS IS THE SAVIOR GOD PROMISED. JESUS IS

Immanuel!

"

Jesus is
GOD'S BELOVED SON

— PRACTICE THE MEMORY VERSE —

For everyone who calls on
the name of the Lord will be saved.

ROMANS 10:13

READ TOGETHER
Matthew 3:16–17

SUMMARIZE TOGETHER
Share something you noticed in today's Scripture reading.

After Jesus was born, He grew up big and strong. But, even though He was the Messiah, He did not start telling people about who He was and who God was until He was much older. When Jesus was about thirty years old, it was finally time for Him to begin His ministry or His mission of telling others the reason why He had come to earth. He began His ministry by being baptized in the Jordan River.

Being baptized is a symbol of faith. Through water, it represents dying to your sins the way Jesus died on the cross and then rising to new life the way Jesus arose from the dead. People choose to be baptized to show the world that they have repented of their sins, been forgiven by Jesus, and now live as someone who has a new life in Jesus.

But Jesus was baptized even though He had never sinned. He didn't need to repent. He didn't need forgiveness. So, why was Jesus baptized? Jesus was baptized because He wanted to show us that baptism is an important part of living for God. Jesus was baptized because He was being obedient to His Father.

When Jesus came up out of the water, the heavens opened, and the Spirit of God descended on Him. God the Father also spoke from heaven, saying, "This is my beloved Son, with whom I am well-pleased" (Matthew 3:17). At this moment, all three persons of God—the Father, the Son, and the Holy Spirit—were present together. They were letting everyone know that Jesus really and truly was the promised Savior. He was both God and man. And because He chose to be baptized, even when He didn't need to be, God was so happy with Him. Jesus is holy, which means He is perfect, but He is also humble, which means He is willing to do whatever God asks Him to do. Jesus is God's Son, and God is pleased with Jesus.

Discuss Together

+ Have you been baptized?

+ Why do you think it is important for Christians to be baptized?

Pray Together

+ **THANK** God for sending Jesus to be our example of how to obey.

+ **ASK** God to help you obey Him.

Jesus is
THE MASTER

For everyone who calls on
the name of the Lord will be saved.

ROMANS 10:13

READ TOGETHER
Luke 5:5–10

SUMMARIZE TOGETHER
Share something you noticed in today's Scripture reading.

Think of a time when you worked together with a team or group. Have you done a school project with other students? Have you played on a sports team or joined a musical ensemble? Jesus also worked together with a team to help spread the news that He was the Savior, and God was going to do something big through Him. Jesus carefully picked each person on His team and called them His disciples—only, He didn't pick the strongest, smartest, richest, and most talented men. He picked regular guys. Some of them were outcasts or people who didn't have a lot of friends. Some of them were caught up in making bad choices before they met Jesus. But Jesus knew what He was doing. He knew these men were the perfect ones to be on His team.

Simon Peter, James, and John were among the first men Jesus called to be His disciples. They were all fishermen, but one day when Jesus came to talk to them, they were having a hard time catching any fish. They had been fishing all night and had not caught anything! They must have been very tired and very discouraged. But Jesus told them to cast their nets and try one more time. They did, and this time, they caught so many fish that their heavy nets started to sink the boat! Can you imagine how many fish that must have been?

Simon Peter was amazed at what Jesus had done! He fell to his knees and told Jesus he was not worthy of such a blessing because he was just a sinner. But Jesus already knew Simon Peter was a sinner, and yet, He still wanted Simon Peter to be His disciple. He called Simon Peter and his fishing partners, James and John, to leave behind their life as fishermen and instead follow Him and learn how to be fishers of men. Simon Peter, James, and John knew there was something remarkable about Jesus! Even though their jobs as fishermen provided food and money for them, they knew that Jesus would provide for them if they followed Him as their Master. They trusted Jesus and gave up everything to be Jesus's disciples because they knew Jesus was worth it!

Simon Peter, James, and John knew there was something remarkable about Jesus!

Discuss Together

+ How many fish did the fishermen catch on their own? How many did they catch with Jesus?

+ Was Jesus looking for people who were perfect to be His disciples?

Pray Together

+ **THANK** God for loving imperfect people.

+ **ASK** God to help you say "yes" when He calls you to obey and follow Him.

"

Jesus is
THE MASTER!

"

Jesus is
THE HEALER

For everyone who calls on
the name of the Lord will be saved.

ROMANS 10:13

READ TOGETHER
Mark 2:2–5

SUMMARIZE TOGETHER
Share something you noticed in today's Scripture reading.

One of Jesus's most important missions while He was on earth was to show people what God's kingdom looks like. Ever since Adam and Eve sinned, the whole earth had been full of pain. People were sick, they lied, and they hurt one another. The earth was the kingdom of darkness, the kingdom of sin. But Jesus was bringing a new kingdom, the kingdom of God. And He was the leader of this kingdom. God's kingdom was different. It was full of healing, hope, forgiveness for sins, and love. Jesus showed people what God's kingdom was like, one act at a time.

One day, while Jesus was teaching a big group, a few men decided to bring their sick friend to Jesus to see if He could heal him. Their friend could not walk. The men carried their friend to Jesus, but when they got to the place Jesus was, there were so many people that they could not get to Jesus! They couldn't give up, though.

Their friend needed Jesus. He was the only One who could heal his legs. So they decided to do something crazy. They climbed onto the roof of the home Jesus was in. And they dug a hole right through the roof! Once the hole was big enough, they tied ropes onto their friend's bed and lowered him down through the roof until he was right in front of Jesus.

You would think Jesus would have been mad that they put a hole in the roof, but He wasn't. No, He wasn't upset at all. Instead, Jesus saw how the men believed so much in His power to heal that they would do anything to bring their friend to Him. Jesus saw their faith. And then Jesus said to the sick man, "Son, your sins are forgiven," and "Get up, take up your mat, and go home" (Mark 2:5, 11). Jesus healed the man's heart that was sick with sin, and He healed the man's legs. Immediately, the man got up and walked. It was a miracle! Everyone was amazed and praised God. Jesus was showing everyone that, in God's kingdom, all that is wrong will be made right. Jesus was showing that He was the healer, not only for this man but for all people.

> Jesus was showing that He was the healer, not only for this man but for all people.

Discuss Together

+ Why do you think the men made a hole in the roof?

+ What two things did Jesus do for the man who was sick?

Pray Together

+ **THANK** God for sending Jesus to be our healer.

+ **ASK** God to heal any sickness you have.

Faith: Believing that Jesus is real and trusting that He can save you from your sin

"

JESUS SHOWED PEOPLE WHAT GOD'S KINGDOM WAS LIKE,

one act at a time.

"

Jesus is the
LEADER OF THE
UPSIDE-DOWN KINGDOM

— PRACTICE THE MEMORY VERSE —

For everyone who calls on
the name of the Lord will be saved.

ROMANS 10:13

READ TOGETHER
Matthew 5:2–5

SUMMARIZE TOGETHER
Share something you noticed in today's Scripture reading.

Imagine with me that, all of a sudden, everything flipped upside down. You could walk on the ceiling, and cars could drive in the sky. You could read books upside down and even sleep upside down! That would be crazy, right?

Jesus once taught about an upside-down kingdom. But it wasn't the same kind of upside-down we just imagined. No, everyone still walked on the ground, and everything was still right side up. Jesus's kingdom was upside-down in other ways. He said that the smallest people, the least important people, and the people no one liked to be around were actually the most important people. And people who were quiet and gentle were actually the strongest. He even said that those who seemed to have it all together and looked perfect on the outside, well, those people were usually the ones who were the weakest and poorest. This might not seem to make a lot of sense. But, that's because when we look at people, we see what's on the outside. We think someone who is tall and has big muscles is strong. But Jesus looks at people's hearts. He said the people who realize they are small and weak and ask for God's help are the people who are truly the strong ones.

Everyone was amazed listening to Jesus. All along, they had thought that it was what was on the outside that counted. But Jesus told them that it was actually what was on the inside that mattered. He told everyone that God's kingdom wasn't at all like any other kingdom. To be important in God's kingdom, you had to pursue being unimportant. Jesus told everyone to serve and love one another. He even said we should love people who are unloving toward us. God's kingdom is upside-down. It isn't about being the biggest and best—it is about being like Jesus. Jesus is the leader of God's upside-down kingdom.

Jesus looks at people's hearts.

Discuss Together

+ What are some of the ways the world describes someone who is strong? What about someone who is happy? Or important?

+ How does Jesus describe these people?

Pray Together

+ **THANK** God for teaching us about His kingdom through Jesus.

+ **ASK** God to help you serve and love people as Jesus does.

"

Jesus is

THE LEADER OF GOD'S UPSIDE-DOWN KINGDOM.

"

Jesus is the
BREAD OF LIFE

For everyone who calls on
the name of the Lord will be saved.

ROMANS 10:13

READ TOGETHER
John 6:8-12, 35

SUMMARIZE TOGETHER
Share something you noticed in today's Scripture reading.

One day, Jesus was teaching a very, very big crowd of people and realized they were getting hungry. But the place where Jesus was teaching the crowd was far away from anywhere they could get some food. Jesus told His disciples to feed the people. The disciples told Jesus there was no food! They couldn't feed anyone! Then, Andrew found a young boy who was carrying a small lunch and joked that they could feed the giant crowd with only the two loaves and five fish the boy had. But Andrew's joke actually wasn't a joke at all. Jesus did take the boy's very small lunch, and after He prayed, He broke the bread and shared it with everyone.

Somehow, that tiny lunch fed a huge crowd of five thousand men—and that's not even counting the women and children who were likely gathered there, too! Some believe Jesus fed as many as fifteen thousand people that day. Everyone was amazed. How could Jesus have done this? This was a miracle! There was even some food leftover at the end. Can you believe it?

The next day, the crowd followed Jesus as He traveled to a new place. They were hoping He could feed them another miraculous meal. But this time, Jesus fed them in a different way. He told them, "I am the bread of life. No one who comes to me will ever be hungry, and no one who believes in me will ever be thirsty again." The people were confused. They wanted lunch, but Jesus wasn't going to feed them lunch today. Instead, He wanted to give them something better. He wanted to feed their hearts.

All people have a desire in their hearts to know God and be connected to God. You and I both have this desire. Jesus was telling the people that He was the bread that would satisfy the craving of their hearts to be near to God. Just like the lunch He gave them filled their bellies, He was speaking truth to them that would fill their hearts. Jesus said He is the Bread of Life. When Jesus died on the cross, He took the punishment for the sins of all people. And, because He forgives the sins of all who believe in Him, those who believe can be close to God. Our longing to know God is fulfilled through Jesus. Jesus is the Bread of Life.

All people have a desire in their hearts to know God and be connected to God.

Discuss Together

+ Do you ever wonder who made you, who made the world, or for what purpose you were born? How do these questions point you to God?

+ What do you think it means that Jesus is the Bread of Life?

Pray Together

+ **THANK** God for sending Jesus to give life to all who believe in Him.

+ **ASK** God to help you see that Jesus fulfills the desires of your heart.

"

OUR LONGING TO KNOW GOD IS FULFILLED THROUGH JESUS.

JESUS IS

the Bread of Life.

"

Jesus is the
LIGHT OF THE WORLD

— PRACTICE THE MEMORY VERSE —

For everyone who calls on
the name of the Lord will be saved.

ROMANS 10:13

READ TOGETHER

John 1:9, John 8:12

SUMMARIZE TOGETHER

Share something you noticed in today's Scripture reading.

How do you feel about the dark? Does it make you feel afraid? Darkness can be scary because, in it, we cannot see our surroundings. We want to turn on the lights so we can see clearly! The Bible describes the world as a dark place—and not just dark at night when the sun has set but dark because sin is everywhere. Sin separates us from God. It makes it so we cannot see the world as God intended it to be, and instead, we only see the bad things. Yet God did not want His people to be in the dark, so He sent Jesus to light up the world!

In John 8:12, the people were having a big party to celebrate the goodness of God. They were having a celebration to remember when their ancestors escaped from Egypt and lived in the wilderness. During that time, God provided shelter, food, and even light for them! God sent a big pillar of fire to light their wilderness camp at night. This was a sign that God was with them, and He was going to take care of them. Though the desert wilderness was dark and scary, God's fire and light comforted them. To remember this time, they would light big lanterns, and as the lanterns shone in the darkness, they remembered how God's fire shone in the desert so long ago.

It was during this party—when the lanterns were lit and everyone was remembering how God gave them light in the wilderness—that Jesus said, "I am the light of the world" (John 8:12)! God had sent fire to light up the dark night for His people long ago. And now, He had sent Jesus to light up the darkness sin caused. Jesus told the people that whoever followed Him would never walk in darkness. This means that anyone who believes in Him will be forgiven of their sins and will have the light of life instead of the darkness of sin. Jesus changed everything. Though the world was dark with sin, Jesus is the Light of the World!

> God did not want His people to be in the dark, so He sent Jesus to light up the world!

Discuss Together

+ Why do you think the Bible often describes sin as darkness?

+ John 1:5 says, "That light shines in the darkness, and yet the darkness did not overcome it." What do you think is stronger—Jesus's light or the darkness of sin?

Pray Together

+ **THANK** God for sending Jesus to be our light.

+ **ASK** God to help you look to Jesus as your light when life seems dark.

"

THOUGH THE WORLD WAS DARK WITH SIN, JESUS IS

the Light
of the World!

"

Jesus is the
COMMANDER OF THE WIND AND WAVES

— PRACTICE THE MEMORY VERSE —

For everyone who calls on
the name of the Lord will be saved.

ROMANS 10:13

READ TOGETHER
Luke 8:22–25

SUMMARIZE TOGETHER
Share something you noticed in today's Scripture reading.

In the place where Jesus and His disciples lived, there was a big stretch of water, called the Sea of Galilee, that had loud, scary storms. When there was a storm on the lake, boats would be tossed between giant waves while rain poured down and the wind roared and howled. One of these storms happened while Jesus and His disciples were in a boat on the lake, and the disciples were very worried! They were afraid their boat would overturn, and they would be thrown into the raging waters. We can imagine that they must have been crying, shouting, and very upset!

But Jesus, who was right there in the boat with them, was not upset or scared. In fact, He was not even awake. He was napping. How could Jesus be sleeping at a time like this? The disciples could not understand, so they woke Jesus up and told Him, "We're going to die!" (Luke 8:24). What do you think Jesus did? Did He start crying and shouting, too? No. Jesus got up, and He spoke to the wind and the waves. He told them to stop storming and be calm. And they did! Immediately, the waves died down, and the wind stopped blowing. Then, He turned to His disciples, and He asked them, "Where is your faith?" (Luke 8:25).

The disciples were so scared of the storm that they forgot Jesus had already told them something important about their journey. Before they set out on the water, He had told them they would cross over to the other side (Luke 8:22). The storm made them doubt what Jesus had said. Somewhere deep inside of them, they must have believed the wind was strong enough to stop what Jesus said from coming true. When Jesus calmed the wind and the waves, He showed the disciples that He is stronger. He is in control of the entire world! Jesus is still this strong today. There is nothing and no one that can stop what He says from happening. Jesus is the commander of the wind and the waves!

> When Jesus calmed the wind and the waves, He showed the disciples that He is stronger.

Discuss Together

+ The disciples doubted Jesus. Do you ever have a hard time believing the things Jesus has said to you through the Bible?

+ List some things that Jesus is stronger than.

Pray Together

+ **THANK** God for being strong and sending His strong Son, Jesus, to us.

+ **ASK** God to help you trust His strength.

"
Jesus is the
COMMANDER
OF THE WIND AND
THE WAVES!
"

Jesus is the
GOOD SHEPHERD

— PRACTICE THE MEMORY VERSE —

For everyone who calls on
the name of the Lord will be saved.

ROMANS 10:13

READ TOGETHER
John 10:14–15

SUMMARIZE TOGETHER
Share something you noticed in today's Scripture reading.

Do you know what a shepherd is? A shepherd is someone who cares for a flock of sheep. The shepherd protects the sheep from wild animals and other dangers. He also makes sure the sheep have food and water. If a sheep is hurt, the shepherd helps it heal. If a sheep is lost, the shepherd will find it and bring it back home. Sheep need shepherds to be their caretakers!

Jesus tells us that He is the Good Shepherd who cares for His people just like a shepherd cares for his sheep. Jesus leads and guides His people through the Holy Spirit. He provides the spiritual food we need to grow in our faith. If we are weak, struggling, or feeling far away from Him, He finds and helps us. Jesus keeps His people safe by promising them eternal life in Him. Everyone needs someone to take care of their spiritual needs. We all have sin, and sin separates us from God. Jesus's death and resurrection have made a way for us to be forgiven and come close to God. Jesus is our spiritual caretaker! And in order for Him to care for us, He had to go so far as to give His life on the cross. Yet He did this willingly because He knew it was what was required to take care of our sins. This is why Jesus isn't just a shepherd—He is the Good Shepherd!

Something amazing about Jesus as the Good Shepherd is that He knows each and every one of His people by name. A shepherd is careful to count each and every sheep in their herd so that none are lost or forgotten. And Jesus does the same. He never leaves behind or forgets any of His people. Every person who chooses to believe in Jesus and asks Him to forgive their sins is part of Jesus's flock of sheep. Jesus will always care for His flock. He will be by their side always and lead them into eternal life in heaven with Him. Isn't that amazing? Jesus is the Good Shepherd!

Jesus keeps His people safe by promising them eternal life in Him.

Discuss Together

+ What do you think it looks like for Jesus to care for His people as their Shepherd?

+ How does it make you feel that Jesus gave His life so that He could take care of your sins and offer your forgiveness?

Pray Together

+ **THANK** Jesus for laying down His life for His people.

+ **ASK** God to help you recognize and follow the leading of Jesus the Good Shepherd.

" JESUS WILL *always care* FOR HIS FLOCK. "

Jesus is the
WAY, TRUTH, AND LIFE

— PRACTICE THE MEMORY VERSE —

For everyone who calls on
the name of the Lord will be saved.

ROMANS 10:13

READ TOGETHER
John 14:6

SUMMARIZE TOGETHER
Share something you noticed in today's Scripture reading.

There has never been anyone like Jesus who has walked on the earth. Jesus is not only a man, but He is also God. He taught people about God with boldness. He performed many amazing miracles. He loved people with perfect love. But Jesus's mission when He came to the earth was not only to do these things. His mission also involved Him giving His life to pay for the sins of all people. So, after a while of teaching, performing miracles, and loving people, Jesus told His disciples the time was coming when He would have to go away.

The disciples were confused. Where was Jesus going? When was He leaving? Why did He have to go? They wanted Him to stay. But Jesus couldn't stay. He had to obey what God was asking Him to do. And God was asking Him to die on a cross. A few days before it was time for Jesus to die, He gathered His disciples to teach them something very important. He told them, "I am the way, the truth, and the life. No one comes to the Father except through me" (John 14:6).

What did Jesus mean when He said He was the way, the truth, and the life? Jesus meant that He and only He could make a way for people to get to God. Many times, we have talked about all the ways people tried to get to God, but they were never able to get there on their own. Jesus said He would make a way.

Jesus also said He is the truth. God had given His people a lot of rules to keep, but they had never been able to keep them. Jesus, however, kept all the rules perfectly. He lived a life that was true to what God said was right and good. Jesus is the truth. And He is also the life. Jesus gives life to all things. And not only does He give life to things here on earth, but He gives forever spiritual life to those who believe in Him. That means that anyone who believes in Jesus will live forever with Him. There has never been and there never will be anyone else like Jesus. He is the way, the truth, and the life!

There has never been and there never will be anyone else like Jesus.

Discuss Together

+ Think back to the time we've spent going through this devotional together. Do you remember some of the ways that people tried to get to God on their own? Were they able to get to God? *Hint: Check out pages 38 (Jesus Is the Only Way to God), 62 (Jesus Is the Perfect Sacrifice), and 96 (Jesus Is the Rebuilder).*

+ How do you think Jesus's disciples felt when they learned He was going to die soon?

Pray Together

+ **THANK** God for making a way to Him through Jesus.

+ **ASK** God to help you understand the truth and life found in Jesus.

"

ANYONE WHO BELIEVES IN JESUS WILL
live forever
WITH HIM.

"

Jesus is the
CRUCIFIED SON OF GOD

For everyone who calls on
the name of the Lord will be saved.

ROMANS 10:13

READ TOGETHER
Luke 22:2-6, 23:33-34, 23:44-46

SUMMARIZE TOGETHER
Share something you noticed in today's Scripture reading.

Have you ever received a consequence you didn't deserve? Maybe a parent made you clean a mess that one of your siblings made because they thought you did it. Or possibly a teacher at school told you to stop talking in class, but really it was your friend next to you who was the one talking. Receiving a consequence that you don't deserve is unfair and feels really frustrating. However, taking on an undeserved consequence is exactly what Jesus did. Today, we will discuss the day when Jesus took on the consequences for all the sins that anyone ever has or ever will commit. Romans 6:23 tells us that the punishment for sin is death. All people sin and deserve death. But Jesus never sinned, and therefore, He did not deserve to die. Instead, He chose to die for us.

Even though Jesus never did anything wrong, there were people called the Pharisees, who believed Jesus was lying about being God's son. These people arrested Jesus, beat Jesus, and made fun of Jesus. They put a sharp crown of thorns on His head and laughed at Him. Then, they sentenced Him to the most painful death possible—death on a cross. They drove big spike-like nails through His hands and feet, and they pierced His side with a sword. Jesus's mother, His friends, and His disciples watched as Jesus breathed His last breath and died.

When Jesus died, two mysterious things happened. The first was that the sun stopped shining, and it was dark. The light of life had died. The second thing was that in the place where the Jews worshiped, a curtain that had been hanging for hundreds of years to separate God's presence from the people was torn in two! What could this mean? It meant that Jesus had once and for all paid the price for sin. Now, all people who trust in Jesus could be near to God because Jesus had taken care of their sin problem. Now that Jesus was dead, His disciples wondered what would happen next. They didn't understand why Jesus had to die. But soon and very soon they would understand. Jesus's work on earth was not done yet!

All people who trust in Jesus could be near to God because Jesus had taken care of their sin problem.

Discuss Together

+ What is the consequence that everyone is given by God for their sin?

+ Who took care of the consequences God should give you because of your sin?

+ Romans 10:9 says, "If you confess with your mouth, 'Jesus is Lord,' and believe in your heart that God raised him from the dead, you will be saved." And Romans 10:13 says, "For everyone who calls on the name of the Lord will be saved." What must you do to be saved from your sins?

Pray Together

Grown-ups: this may be a great time to refer to *Sharing the Good News of the Gospel with Children* on pages 16-17.

+ **THANK** God for making a way for your sins to be forgiven through Jesus.

+ **ASK** God to forgive your sins.

"

JESUS HAD

once and for all

PAID THE PRICE
FOR SIN.

"

Jesus is the
RISEN SAVIOR

For everyone who calls on
the name of the Lord will be saved.

ROMANS 10:13

READ TOGETHER
Luke 24:2–7, 36–39, 49–51

SUMMARIZE TOGETHER
Share something you noticed in today's Scripture reading.

After Jesus died, His body was laid in a tomb. Three days later, two women came to prepare Jesus's body to be buried. Only, Jesus's body wasn't there! These two women likely thought, *Oh no, this is terrible! What has happened to Jesus's body?* Suddenly, two angels appeared and told the women that Jesus's body was gone because He was not dead anymore—He had risen from the dead! They could not believe what they were hearing! Could it be that Jesus had come back to life?

Yes, it was true! Jesus appeared to the women, His disciples, and many other people to show that He had not stayed dead but had resurrected from the dead. Some people were very glad! Others were shocked. Some didn't believe it could possibly be true. But Jesus showed them His hands and feet. They saw the scars from where the nails had pierced His skin, and they believed that He was really Jesus, the risen Savior.

Jesus spent some time with His disciples and others who believed in Him. He taught them about the reasons He came and how He had fulfilled all of the promises that God made in the Old Testament about the Messiah. Jesus also told them to share the good news that He would forgive people's sins if they believed in Him.

Jesus lived on the earth for forty days after His resurrection. When that time was up, He went back to His Father in heaven and sat down at His right hand there. Before He ascended and went back to heaven, Jesus gave His followers a promise. Jesus promised His followers that He was sending them something special and powerful to help them very soon. The people watched Jesus rise to heaven as they worshiped Him because He was the risen Savior! Then, they went back to Jerusalem and waited to receive the promise.

Jesus promised His followers that He was sending them something special and powerful to help them very soon.

Discuss Together

+ Why do you think some people had a hard time believing that Jesus was alive again? What did Jesus do to help them believe?

+ Read Isaiah 25:8 below. Which is stronger: death or Jesus?

*When he has swallowed up death once and for all,
the Lord God will wipe away the tears
from every face
and remove his people's disgrace
from the whole earth,
for the Lord has spoken.*

Pray Together

+ **THANK** God for being strong and mighty.

+ **ASK** God to help you trust Him in moments of doubt.

Heaven: The place where God, Jesus, and other heavenly beings (like angels) live

"

THE PEOPLE WATCHED JESUS RISE TO HEAVEN AS THEY WORSHIPED HIM BECAUSE HE WAS *the risen Savior!*

"

Seeing Jesus in

ACTS–REVELATION

Memory Verse

Our citizenship is in heaven,
and we eagerly wait
for a Savior from there,
the Lord Jesus Christ.

PHILIPPIANS 3:20

Jesus is the
SENDER OF
THE HOLY SPIRIT

— PRACTICE THE MEMORY VERSE —

Our citizenship is in heaven, and we eagerly wait
for a Savior from there, the Lord Jesus Christ.

PHILIPPIANS 3:20

READ TOGETHER
Acts 1:8; 2:1–2

SUMMARIZE TOGETHER
Share something you noticed in today's Scripture reading.

After Jesus left the earth to go back to heaven, His disciples didn't
know what would happen next. Jesus had told them to share the
good news about Him dying on the cross to forgive sin, but He also
told them to stay in Jerusalem. He told them to stay because He
was going to send the Holy Spirit, who would make them strong and
brave enough to tell the whole world about Jesus. So the disciples,
who were also called apostles, waited.

One day, while the apostles were praying with many others who
believed in Jesus, the whole room was filled with a loud sound, like
a mighty wind was blowing straight from heaven and into the room
they were in. They saw flames of fire in the air, and the flames rested
on each person, but they did not hurt them. The wind and the fire

were the Holy Spirit. Just like God the Father is God and Jesus is God, the Holy Spirit is also God.

Now that Jesus had returned to heaven, the Holy Spirit came down to earth to help God's people. The Holy Spirit immediately started helping them spread the message about the wonderful things Jesus had done. He helped them speak in languages they didn't know, so they could tell people from far away places about Jesus. He made them brave, so they could talk to big crowds about Jesus. And He helped them do many miracles, just like Jesus had done.

Jesus had left the earth, but He had not left His people alone. The Holy Spirit came to continue the work Jesus started. And the amazing thing is that the Holy Spirit is still here today! He lives in every single person who trusts Jesus to be their Savior. The Holy Spirit leads, guides, helps, and comforts God's people. Because Jesus has forgiven our sins, God can come so close to us that He can even live inside of us through the Holy Spirit. Jesus is the sender of the Holy Spirit!

The Holy Spirit leads, guides, helps, and comforts God's people.

Discuss Together

+ John 14:26 says, "But the Counselor, the Holy Spirit, whom the Father will send in my name, will teach you all things and remind you of everything I have told you." What does Jesus say the Holy Spirit does in this verse?

+ Have you ever experienced the help of the Holy Spirit?

Pray Together

+ **THANK** God that He gave us the Holy Spirit.

+ **ASK** God to help you hear the leading of the Holy Spirit.

"

THE HOLY SPIRIT CAME TO
continue the work
JESUS STARTED.

"

Jesus is
THE WAY TO
PEACE WITH GOD

— PRACTICE THE MEMORY VERSE —

Our citizenship is in heaven, and we eagerly wait
for a Savior from there, the Lord Jesus Christ.

PHILIPPIANS 3:20

READ TOGETHER
Romans 5:1–2

SUMMARIZE TOGETHER
Share something you noticed in today's Scripture reading.

After Jesus died, rose again, and went back to heaven, His followers
knew the most important thing they could do was to tell everyone
about Jesus. God had promised so long ago to Abraham, Moses,
and David that He was going to send a Savior. And He did! Now,
anyone who believed in Jesus was forgiven of their sins and was able
to enter into a relationship with God. This was amazing news!

But some people wondered if Jesus had come to save everyone or
if He had only come to save people who were in the family of Abraham. After all, God's promise to Abraham, way back in Genesis 15,
was that God would protect and care for his family. Those who were
in Abraham's family were called Jews. People not in Abraham's family
were called Gentiles. God wanted the good news about Jesus to go

to everyone, both Jews and Gentiles. It didn't matter what family you were born into, where you lived, or what you looked like. Anyone could become a part of God's family—they only needed to have faith in Jesus.

God used a man named Paul to tell the Gentiles that Jesus had died for their sins, and they could be a part of God's family. Paul told people they could not earn God's grace, no matter how hard they tried. God just gives it away for free to anyone who believes. Paul knew a lot about this grace, as he had done a lot of wrong things. Yet God graciously forgave him and asked him to tell others about this amazing grace. Paul spent his life telling people that Jesus paid for our sins and, because of that, they could have peace with God. Jesus—and Jesus alone—is the way to peace with God.

> God wanted the good news about Jesus to go to everyone, both Jews and Gentiles.

Discuss Together

+ Can we earn God's forgiveness by being good?

+ How do we find peace with God?

Pray Together

+ **THANK** God for sending Jesus to pay for your sin so that God could forgive you.

+ **ASK** God to help you trust that peace with Him comes through Jesus.

"

JESUS—AND JESUS ALONE— IS THE WAY TO *peace with God.*

"

Jesus is
THE HEAD
OF THE CHURCH

— PRACTICE THE MEMORY VERSE —

Our citizenship is in heaven, and we eagerly wait
for a Savior from there, the Lord Jesus Christ.

PHILIPPIANS 3:20

READ TOGETHER

1 Corinthians 12:4–6, 27

SUMMARIZE TOGETHER

Share something you noticed in today's Scripture reading.

What is your favorite gift you have ever received? Did you know that God gives gifts to each person who believes in Jesus and is saved from their sin? He does! The Holy Spirit lives inside of everyone who has put their faith in Jesus. Part of what the Holy Spirit does in people is He helps them grow God's Church. God's Church is more than just a building you go to on Sunday mornings. God's Church is made up of all the people who believe in Jesus across the whole world. God calls His Church the body of Christ.

While Jesus was on earth, He did everything God told Him to do. And many people came to know God through the things Jesus did and said. Now that Jesus is in heaven, God's people, His Church, are the ones God uses to tell people about Him. The Holy Spirit gives each person special gifts that we should use to tell people about Jesus. Some people are great singers, others love to teach, some are artistic, some are compassionate, and still others love to help anyone who needs it.

No matter what your gift is, the body of Christ needs you! Just like every part of your body is important, so every person who believes in Jesus is an important part of the body of Christ. There is no person who is more important than the others. The purpose of the body of Christ is to share the good news about Jesus with the whole world. The body of Christ is God's plan to share the message of Jesus with the world! Each person in the body of Christ should do two things. First is the most important thing—they should follow Jesus's lead. And second, they should do their part so that the whole body can be made strong. The most important part of the body of Christ is Jesus. Just as your brain tells your whole body what to do, Jesus tells the body of Christ what to do and how to move. Jesus is the head of the body of Christ and the Church.

> The Holy Spirit gives each person special gifts that we should use to tell people about Jesus.

Discuss Together

+ What is a gift God gave you to make the body of Christ strong? (*Grown-ups, this is a great chance to discuss your child's strengths and talents with them!*)

+ What is the most important thing you can do as part of the body of Christ?

Pray Together

+ **THANK** God for giving us Jesus to lead the Church.

+ **ASK** God to help you use your gifts to make His Church strong.

"

THE BODY OF CHRIST IS GOD'S PLAN TO SHARE THE MESSAGE OF JESUS
with the world!

"

Jesus is
THE GREATEST
TREASURE

— PRACTICE THE MEMORY VERSE —

Our citizenship is in heaven, and we eagerly wait
for a Savior from there, the Lord Jesus Christ.

PHILIPPIANS 3:20

READ TOGETHER
Philippians 3:7–9

SUMMARIZE TOGETHER
Share something you noticed in today's Scripture reading.

What do you think makes a person important? Are they important
if they are big and strong? Or are they important if they have the
nicest and newest clothes? Maybe it is if they follow all the rules and
do all the right things? Paul was a man who had tried his whole life
to be someone important. And he didn't just want to be important
in the eyes of other people, but he also wanted to be important in
the eyes of God. He was born into an important family. His parents
followed all of God's rules, and so did he as he grew up. Paul worked
so hard to be a good person so that God would love and accept him.
He was so proud of all of the good things he had done!

Then, Paul met Jesus. And he realized that being accepted and
loved by God had nothing to do with which family you were part of

and how many of the rules you followed. Being accepted by God only required one thing: faith in Jesus. You had to believe that you were a sinner, that Jesus paid the price for your sins, and that God would forgive your sins and accept you because of what Jesus had done—not because of what you had done. Paul couldn't believe it! He had been wrong this whole time.

All of a sudden, the long list of good things Paul had done wasn't important to him anymore. Those things didn't matter very much at all. What mattered was Jesus. Paul wanted to learn more about Jesus and obey Jesus and make Jesus the most important person in his life. Why? Because Jesus had done the most amazing thing for Paul when He died for his sins! Paul called all of his accomplishments worthless when he compared them with what it was like to know Jesus. Paul realized that Jesus was the greatest treasure! And because Jesus was the greatest treasure, Paul stopped trying to be so important. He knew now he could not be important on his own. But through Jesus, Paul was accepted and loved by God!

But through Jesus, Paul was
accepted and loved by God!

Discuss Together

+ Does God love and accept people because of the good things they do?

+ At first, Paul made his whole life about doing the right things. Then, he changed and made his whole life about serving and loving Jesus. Why do you think Paul made that change?

Pray Together

+ **THANK** God that you do not have to earn His love by doing the right things.

+ **ASK** God to help you love Jesus more than anything else.

> # PAUL REALIZED THAT JESUS WAS THE
> *greatest treasure!*

Jesus is
OUR STRENGTH

— PRACTICE THE MEMORY VERSE —

Our citizenship is in heaven, and we eagerly wait
for a Savior from there, the Lord Jesus Christ.

PHILIPPIANS 3:20

READ TOGETHER

2 Thessalonians 3:3–5

SUMMARIZE TOGETHER

Share something you noticed in today's Scripture reading.

Has anyone ever made fun of you or said hurtful words to you because of your faith in Jesus? Many people who believe in Jesus all
over the world have experienced others harming them with words or
actions. This is called "religious persecution." The Bible tells us about
lots of different churches and groups of people who were persecuted
because of their faith in Jesus. One of these groups lived in Thessalonica. The Jesus followers in Thessalonica called Jesus their Lord and
King because He was! But the rulers of the area didn't like that they
called Jesus "King." They said they already had a king named Caesar,
and they should worship him and not Jesus!

Even though these rulers threatened and hurt the Christians in Thessalonica, the Christians just kept telling everyone that Jesus was the
one true King! Those were some really hard times for the Christians.
Paul wrote them a letter to encourage them to keep loving and serv-

ing Jesus no matter what other people said or did! In this letter, Paul reminded them that even when they experienced hard things, God was faithful. God's faithfulness didn't always look like taking the hard things away, but it did look like Him being with them always!

Paul also prayed that when they were persecuted, they would remember that Jesus was persecuted too! Jesus was teased, unfairly arrested, accused of crimes He did not commit, beaten, and killed. Jesus allowed all these things to happen to Him. He was powerful enough to stop the persecution, but He didn't. Jesus knew that what He was experiencing was hard, but God was with Him. Jesus endured and patiently suffered because He knew His death and resurrection were going to be the way people's sins were forgiven.

We may have times when we are persecuted for our faith. In these times, we can remember that God is always with us, and we can look to Jesus's example of how to patiently endure. God has promised to always provide for everything we need, and we can trust Him. Jesus is our strength while we endure and wait for the end to hard things!

God has promised to always provide for everything we need, and we can trust Him.

Discuss Together

+ Have you experienced persecution?

+ When people persecuted Jesus, he prayed for
  them, saying, "Father, forgive them, because they
  do not know what they are doing" (Luke 23:34).
  How can you follow Jesus's example of how to
  handle persecution?

Pray Together

+ **THANK** God that He is always, always with you.

+ **ASK** God to comfort and strengthen persecuted
  Christians around the world.

Religious Persecution: Harm done to someone
because of their faith

Jesus is our strength

WHILE WE ENDURE AND WAIT FOR THE END TO HARD THINGS!

Jesus is
OUR BLESSED HOPE

Our citizenship is in heaven, and we eagerly wait
for a Savior from there, the Lord Jesus Christ.

PHILIPPIANS 3:20

READ TOGETHER
Titus 2:11–13

SUMMARIZE TOGETHER
Share something you noticed in today's Scripture reading.

Do you know what the word "hope" means? It means "to have a desire for something to happen." Is there something that you are hoping for right now? In life, some of the things we hope for will happen, but others will not. Have you ever hoped for something that didn't happen? When we do not receive the things we hope for, it can make us feel sad, frustrated, and disappointed. The Bible never promises us that we will get everything we hope for, but it does promise that everyone who trusts in Jesus has a blessed hope to look forward to!

When we confess our sins and ask God to forgive us, He forgives us because Jesus has paid the price for our sins. He gives us grace! God's grace not only forgives us from our sins, but it also teaches us how to live godly lives. We will mess up and make mistakes as we try to live godly lives. God will give us more grace when that happens. But one day, Jesus will come again to the earth. When

Jesus comes, He is going to make a lot of really big changes. He is going to get rid of all sin, pain, and sorrow. And He will make it so that we never sin again. We will be righteous! And we will live with Him in heaven forever. We won't have to struggle with our desire to do wrong things anymore. We won't have to experience the pain of someone else doing wrong things to us anymore. We won't be sick. We won't be sad. There will be peace, joy, love, and goodness filling every corner of the world.

Doesn't that sound like the most amazing place to live? That is a real place. It is the new heaven and new earth that Jesus will cause to come to be one day. Everyone who believes in Jesus will get to live in the new heaven and earth for all of eternity. That means for ever and ever and ever and ever and... ever. Forever! How wonderful it is to hope for that day! Jesus is our blessed hope!

God's grace not only forgives us from our sins, but it also teaches us how to live godly lives.

Discuss Together

+ Read Revelation 21:1–4 below. What are some of
the things you are looking forward to in the new
heaven and new earth?

*Then I saw a new heaven and a new earth; for the first
heaven and the first earth had passed away, and the sea
was no more. I also saw the holy city, the new Jerusalem, coming down out of heaven from God, prepared
like a bride adorned for her husband.*

*Then I heard a loud voice from the throne: Look, God's
dwelling is with humanity, and he will live with them.
They will be his peoples, and God himself will be with
them and will be their God. He will wipe away every
tear from their eyes. Death will be no more; grief,
crying, and pain will be no more, because the previous
things have passed away.*

+ How do you think the new heaven and earth will be
different from the earth now?

Pray Together

+ **THANK** God that we have the hope of eternity
in the new heaven and earth.

+ **ASK** God to help you put your hope in Him.

Confess: To be honest with God about your thoughts, feelings, or actions—whether they are good or bad

"

EVERYONE WHO TRUSTS IN JESUS HAS
a blessed hope
TO LOOK FORWARD TO!

"

Jesus is the
PERFECTER OF
OUR FAITH

Our citizenship is in heaven, and we eagerly wait
for a Savior from there, the Lord Jesus Christ.

PHILIPPIANS 3:20

READ TOGETHER
Hebrews 12:1–2

SUMMARIZE TOGETHER
Share something you noticed in today's Scripture reading.

Every story has a beginning, middle, and end. Think of your favorite
movie. How does it start? How does it end? Your story with God
also has a beginning, middle, and a very special, everlasting ending.
It might seem like your story with God started when you first heard
about Him or when you prayed to ask Him to forgive you of your
sins. But your story with God started a long time before that! Your
story with God actually starts with Jesus.

Jesus is called the founder or the pioneer of our faith. That means
that Jesus was the pioneer who made a way for everyone else to
have a relationship with God. Jesus is the leader, the author, and
the originator of our faith. Everyone is invited to have a relationship
with God because Jesus made a way for all sins to be forgiven when

He died on the cross. It is amazing that our faith begins in Jesus! Jesus loves us so much that He took the very first step to be in a relationship with us.

Our story with God doesn't stop when we first come into a relationship with Him. That's just the beginning. It also has a middle and an eternal end. During the middle and the end of our story, Jesus is the perfecter of our faith. Jesus lived a perfect life. He never sinned. Through His death and resurrection, He offers His perfection to us and takes on our sin. He has made a way for all to stand sinless before God.

And one day, when Jesus returns to earth, He will do away with all sin forever. The whole world will be sinless, pure, and full of the goodness of God. Jesus will do this by His power and strength alone. He will defeat sin forever. And we will get to enjoy the beautiful ending to our story for all of eternity. Our story with God never ends! Jesus began our story with God. Jesus perfects the faith He starts in us. And because of Jesus, we will forever get to enjoy being with God. Our faith stories—our stories with God—are all about Jesus. Jesus is the founder and perfecter of our faith!

> Jesus was the pioneer who made a way for everyone else to have a relationship with God.

Discuss Together

+ Who began your story or relationship with God?

+ How will your story or relationship with God end? What is special about this ending?

Pray Together

+ **THANK** God for taking the first step to start a relationship with you.

+ **ASK** God to help you to look forward to eternity with Him.

"
OUR STORY
WITH GOD
never ends!
"

Jesus is LOVE

Our citizenship is in heaven, and we eagerly wait
for a Savior from there, the Lord Jesus Christ.

PHILIPPIANS 3:20

READ TOGETHER

1 John 4:7–8

SUMMARIZE TOGETHER

Share something you noticed in today's Scripture reading.

What is something that makes you feel loved? Is it when your favorite snack is waiting for you when you get home from school? Or when someone sees that you are sad and gives you a hug? It is so nice when people tell us they love us, but we often feel loved the most when they show love with their actions. God chose to show all people that He loved them, not only with His words but also with His actions! To demonstrate His love, God sent Jesus to earth to live a sinless life and yet die for the sins of everyone else.

Jesus shows us God's love because He shows us God's grace. God forgives us of our sins because Jesus took care of the consequences for our sins. God did not have to send Jesus. Jesus did not have to come. Jesus did not have to die. He could have just gone back to heaven without going through the pain and heartache of dying on the cross. But Jesus knew that His mission in coming to earth was to show the love of God to all people. So He willingly suffered and died because of the love He has for the whole world.

God says many times in the Bible that He loves all people. But sometimes, we might read these verses and know these verses but still have a hard time believing God loves us. We might think that if God truly loved us, He would have done things differently in our lives. Or we might think that if He loved others, He would stop all the sad things that happen in the world. Those are really big questions that even lots of grown-ups have a hard time answering.

God is okay with us asking Him hard questions. He will help us when we have doubts or feel confused. But we can also look to Jesus when we question God's love. Jesus showed us, with His willingness to die in our place, that He loves us and God loves us. Jesus loved you enough to die for you. That is the biggest, strongest, most wonderful love that has ever been shown! Jesus is love.

Discuss Together

+ Do you ever have a hard time believing God loves you?

+ How did God show His love for you through Jesus?

Pray Together

+ **THANK** God for His love.

+ **ASK** God to help you see His love for you in action through Jesus.

Jesus is
THE ONE WHO WILL MAKE ALL THINGS NEW

Our citizenship is in heaven, and we eagerly wait for a Savior from there, the Lord Jesus Christ.

PHILIPPIANS 3:20

READ TOGETHER

Revelation 21:3–5

SUMMARIZE TOGETHER

Share something you noticed in today's Scripture reading.

Have you ever had a paper cut? Those little cuts sting and sometimes bleed at first, but eventually, the discomfort stops, and your skin grows back together. Where there once was a painful wound, there will be brand-new, healthy skin. It is amazing that God created our bodies to heal in this way! God also has a plan to heal the whole world of the pain and sorrow sin causes. Jesus saves all those who believe in Him from the consequences they deserve as a result of their sin. Yet, sometimes, we still experience the effects of sin.

If someone lies to us, it causes confusion and hurts our relationship with them. If we choose to gossip about a friend, our words can make our friend upset. Right now on the earth, sin still causes a lot of problems and pain.

But there is a day coming when Jesus will come to the earth for a second time. When He comes again, He is going to defeat Satan and Satan's helpers once and for all. He will lock them away forever. And He will rule and reign as King over the entire earth. In a world where Jesus is King, there is no sin. There is no pain, no suffering, no sickness, and no sorrow. Jesus will make a new heaven and a new earth. He will heal the whole earth from the pain sin causes.

In the new heaven and new earth, God will live with His people once again. He will walk among us, talk with us, and not be separated from us in any way. Anyone who believes in Jesus will live in the new heaven and new earth forever. No one who lives there will ever die. They will have eternal life. God will be with them for all eternity. What an amazing future this is to look forward to! Jesus is the One who will make all things new.

In a world where Jesus is King, there is no sin.

Discuss Together

+ What is something you are looking forward to Jesus making new?

+ What is something hard you are experiencing right now? Does it help you to know that this hard thing you're experiencing is only for a little while, but eternity with Jesus will last forever?

Pray Together

+ **THANK** God that He has a plan to heal the whole world.

+ **ASK** God to send Jesus to come and heal the world soon.

"

ANYONE WHO BELIEVES IN JESUS WILL LIVE IN THE NEW HEAVEN AND NEW EARTH *forever.*

"

The Bible Really is
ALL ABOUT JESUS

Our citizenship is in heaven, and we eagerly wait
for a Savior from there, the Lord Jesus Christ.

PHILIPPIANS 3:20

READ TOGETHER
John 3:16–17

SUMMARIZE TOGETHER
Share something you noticed in today's Scripture reading.

The story of the Bible is the story of God making a way to be in relationship with His people. In the very beginning, Adam and Eve lived in the garden with God. God walked and talked with them. Then their sin separated them from God. And the whole rest of the Bible tells us how God made a way for people to be close to Him once again.

God saved Noah from the flood. He chose Abraham's family to make into a great nation of His own people called the Israelites. He sent Moses to free the Israelites from slavery. God instructed His people and lived with them in the tabernacle and the temple. He gave messages to prophets and empowered kings to lead the nation of Israel. Although God was with His people, they were not as close to Him as He wanted them to be. Their sin separated them from God. And they couldn't fix their sin problem on their own. But God could fix it. God sent Jesus to the earth as Immanuel, which means God with us.

Everywhere Jesus went while He was on the earth, He showed people what God is like. He healed sickness, forgave sin, and taught the truth about God and His kingdom. But people didn't understand who Jesus was, and they sentenced Him to death on a cross. But not even death could stop God's plan to be with His people. Jesus rose again to new life! Jesus's death paid the price for all sin, and His resurrection showed that He was stronger than sin and death. Jesus then went back to His Father in heaven, and God sent the Holy Spirit to instruct and comfort all who believe in Jesus.

Now, everyone who admits they are a sinner who needs the forgiveness of Jesus and believes that Jesus's death paid for their sins gets to come close to God. Jesus was God's plan to fix the problem of sin all along! The message of Jesus's life, death, and resurrection is called the gospel. "Gospel" means "good news." And isn't this the best news you have ever heard? Jesus made a way to God when no one else could. Jesus saves our souls from death and brings us into a new life with God. And this new life doesn't even end when we die. We will live forever with Jesus in the new heaven and new earth. There, we will walk with God and talk with God, and sin will be no more. Jesus is the answer to all of our pain and problems. Jesus is the story of the Bible!

The story of the Bible is the story of God making a way to be in relationship with His people.

Discuss Together

+ In your own words, explain the good news of the gospel.

+ What is one thing you learned through this devotional that you did not know before?

Pray Together

+ **THANK** God for loving us enough to take care of the problem of sin for us through Jesus.

+ **ASK** God to help you grow every day in your love for Him.

Gospel: The good news that salvation comes by grace and through faith in Jesus

" "

Jesus made a way
TO GOD WHEN NO ONE ELSE COULD.

" "

GLOSSARY OF TERMS

Born Again:
Receiving a new spiritual life through
Jesus's forgiveness of sins

Confess:
To be honest with God about your thoughts, feelings,
or actions—whether they are good or bad

Eternal life:
Living forever in God's presence without end

Faith:
Believing that Jesus is real and trusting
that He can save you from your sin

Gospel:
The good news that salvation comes by
grace and through faith in Jesus

Heaven:
The place where God, Jesus, and other
heavenly beings (like angels) live

Old Testament:
The first half of the Bible that records God's rules, the history of His people, and His promises of Jesus

New Testament:
The second half of the Bible that records the life, ministry, death, and resurrection of Jesus, as well as what happened after He returned to heaven

Redeem:
To buy one's freedom

Religious Persecution:
Harm done to someone because of their faith

Sacrifice:
An animal or object given to God to pay the price for sin

Salvation:
God rescuing sinners from sin

Satan:
God's enemy, whose mission is to separate people from God for eternity

Sin:
Thoughts, actions, and beliefs that go against God's rules and ways

Thank you for studying
God's Word with us!

CONNECT WITH US

@thedailygraceco
@dailygracepodcast

CONTACT US

info@thedailygraceco.com

SHARE

#thedailygraceco

VISIT US ONLINE

www.thedailygraceco.com

MORE DAILY GRACE

The Daily Grace App
Daily Grace Podcast